A GUIDE TO
NEW YORK STATE
GOVERNMENT

A GUIDE TO NEW YORK STATE GOVERNMENT

Sixth Edition

THE LEAGUE OF WOMEN VOTERS OF NEW YORK STATE

Mary Jo Fairbanks, Editor

(formerly entitled New York State: A Citizen's Guide)

POLICY STUDIES ASSOCIATES
P.O. Box 337
Croton-on-Hudson, New York 10520

A Guide to New York State Government
by the League of Women Voters of New York State
817 Broadway
New York, NY 10003

Editor-in-Chief: Mary Jo Fairbanks
Managing Editor: Paul Wm. Bradley

Typesetting and formatting by Robert Milstein
Book Design by Paul Wm. Bradley and Robert Milstein
Cover Design by Nomi Silverman
Printed by BookCrafters, Chelsea, Michigan.

The text of this book is set in Palatino. Display type is set in Palatino Bold.

Library of Congress Cataloging in Publication Data

Main entry under title:

A guide to New York State government, 6th edition.
(previously entitled: New York State, a citizen's handbook)

Bibliography: p.
Includes index.
1. New York (State) — Politics and government — 1951—
I. Fairbanks, Mary J. II. League of Women Voters of New York State.

ISBN 0-936826-33-9

Published and distributed for the League of Women Voters of New York State by
Policy Studies Associates (PSA), Croton-on-Hudson, New York. PSA is a division of the
Council on International and Public Affairs, 777 United Nations Plaza, New York, N.Y. 10017.

FOREWORD

This *Guide to New York State Government* first appeared in 1954 under the title *New York State: A Citizen's Handbook.* The League of Women Voters of New York State prepared the handbook to provide an overview of state government in a single publication that would be readily available, comprehensive, and understandable. This latest, sixth, edition follows in that tradition.

The project was an outgrowth of the League's dedication to promoting informed and active citizen participation in government. The League, for the past 70 years, has been encouraging voters to go to the polls and providing them with the background information they need to cast their ballots.

The adage "knowledge is power" is nowhere more applicable than in relation to government. Understanding the responsibilities and functions of the various branches of state government enables citizens to evaluate the performance of their representatives and become advocates for issues of importance to them.

This book has grown from a slim volume to a more than 200 page publication over the past 35 years. The expansion of the information it contains reflects the growth in state government over that period. The State University system has been developed, environment-related agencies have burgeoned, and the New York State Legislature has taken on greater and more complex responsibilities. Albany's Empire State Plaza has transformed the face of the state capital itself. In both appearance and function, Albany has become the center of state government.

The League gratefully acknowledges the contributions made to this project in time, talent, and typing. Mary Jo Fairbanks, Publications Director, served as Editor-in-Chief of this volume, supervising the work of contributing editors, copyeditors and proofreaders, and League specialists: Andrée Marr, Susan Schwardt, Zita Loewe, Evelyn Stock, Lee Nesslage, Ruth Shur, Lenore Banks, Susan Richmond, Helaine Lesnick, Susan Hughson, Anna Bundschuh, Lois Wilson, Sonja Johansen, Lorrie Smith, Lynne Toumey, and Barbara Dobkin.

Paul Wm. Bradley of the League's staff was the catalytic force without whom this edition would not have been possible. Ruth Goldstein deserves immense appreciation for word processing the entire manuscript. Nomi Silverman, a special League friend, created and executed the cover design. Robert Milstein's efforts in computer typesetting and formatting the final camera copy under great time pressure were invaluable. Esther Levy, the League's Executive Director, was helpful with many details.

Specialists outside the League who deserve special thanks include: Abraham M. Lackman, the Director of Fiscal Studies of the New York State Senate Finance Committee, and his staff; Harry J. Willis of the New York State Department of State; Madeline Lewis, Deputy Commissioner, and Mary A. Kadlecek of the New York State Department of Environmental Conservation; Marie Hallenbeck of the New York State Department of Transportation; Robert Allen Carter, Senior Librarian, the New York State

Library; Dennis Shea and Paul Scheele of the Political Science Department, SUNY-Oneonta; Dr. Richard Lerer and Dr. Helene Hanson of Southern Westchester BOCES; Elizabeth Jaffe of the Westchester Putnam School Board Association; and Steven LaFever and Marcia Watson of the New York State Board of Elections.

The League also thanks the many experts and consultants who laid the groundwork in previous editions of this book. We are also pleased to be associated with Policy Studies Associates, who, as our publisher, will help us reach a far wider market with this book. Special thanks to William Coplin, who had the vision to see the possibilities.

We hope *A Guide to New York State Government* will inspire students of state government of all ages to involve themselves in the democratic process by which we are governed. That is the essence of our democracy.

Marion S. Sinek
President
League of Women Voters of New York State

TABLE OF CONTENTS

FOREWORD   v

LIST OF FIGURES   xii

PART I. NEW YORK STATE GOVERNMENT   1

Chapter 1. Introduction to New York State   3

Recent History and Trends   3
The State Constitution   8

Chapter 2. The Executive Branch   13

The Governor   13
    Executive and Administrative Powers   14
    Legislative Powers   15
    Limitations on the Governor's Powers   16
    Political Role of the Governor   16
The Lieutenant-Governor   16
The Attorney General   17
The Comptroller   17
Vacancies   18

Chapter 3. The Judicial Branch   19

Court Structure and Jurisdiction   19
    Appellate Courts   19
        The Court of Appeals   19
        The Appellate Divisions   21
        Appellate Terms of the Supreme Court   22
        County Courts   22
    Trial Courts (Courts of Original Jurisdiction)   23
        The Supreme Court   23
        The County Court   23
        The Family Court   23
        The Surrogate's Court   24
        The Court of Claims   24
    Local Trial Courts (Courts of Original Jurisdiction)   24
        The District Court   24
        Town and Village Courts   25
        City Courts outside New York City   25
    New York City Courts   25
Judicial Selection   26
    Qualifications and Terms of Office   26
        Judges of the Court of Appeals   27
        Appellate Division Justices   27

Supreme Court Justices   28
County Court Judges   28
Family Court Judges   28
Surrogate's Court Judges   29
Court of Claims Judges   29
District Court Judges   29
Town and Village Court Justices   29
City Court Judges outside New York City   29
New York City Civil Court Judges   29
New York City Criminal Court Judges   30
Retirement of Judges and Justices   30
Court Administration   30
Financing the Courts   31
Judicial Discipline   32
Role of the Commission   32
Attorneys   33
Counsel for the Indigent   34
The Jury   34
Trial Juries—Civil and Criminal   35
Juror Fees   38
Enforcement   38

Chapter 4. The Legislative Branch   39

Powers and Limitations of the Legislature   39
The Legislators   40
Sessions of the Legislature   41
Organization of the Legislature   43
The Officers   43
The Committees   44

Chapter 5. How a Bill Becomes Law   47

Who May Introduce Bills   47
Schedule for Introducing Bills   49
The Progress of a Bill   49
Obstacles to the Progress of Bills   50
Passing the Bills   51
Counting the Vote   52
Action by the Governor   53
Constitutional Amendments   53

Chapter 6. State Finances   55

Budget Making   55
State Income and Expenditures   58
What the Budget Pays For   60
Borrowing   64
Public Authorities   66
Lease Purchase   69

PART II. LOCAL GOVERNMENT   71

Chapter 7. How Municipalities Operate   73

Home Rule   73
State-Local Fiscal Relationships   74
Local Government Expenditures   75
Property Tax   75
State and Federal Aid   76
Permissive Taxes   78
Special Charges, Fees, and Earnings   78
Equalization and Assessment   79
    Assessment   79
    Equalization   80
State-Local Administrative Relationships   80
The Counties   81
The Cities   84
New York City   86
The Towns   89
The Villages   91
Town-Villages   92
Regional Governments   92

Chapter 8. Local Districts and Authorities   97

School Districts   97
Fire Districts and Fire Protection Districts   97
    Fire Districts   98
    Fire Protection Districts   98
Improvement Districts   99
    County Improvement Districts   99
    Town Improvement Districts   99
Public Authorities   100

PART III. SERVICES TO STATE RESIDENTS   101

Chapter 9. Education in New York State   103

Financing Education   104
State Structure of Education   107
The Board of Regents   107
Department of Education   108
State-Local Relationships   108
BOCES   108
State University of New York (SUNY) System   109

Chapter 10. Social and Human Services   111

Health   113
Mental Hygiene   115
Labor   118
    Wages and Working Conditions   119
    Work Force Services   119
    Labor Relations   121
  Housing   122

Chapter 11. Environment and Public Services   125

Environmental Conservation   125
    Administration   125
    Environmental Quality   126
        Air Resources   126
    Water Quality and Quantity   129
    Solid and Hazardous Waste   130
    Natural Resources Management   133
        Fish and Wildlife   133
        Lands and Forests   134
        Marine Resources   135
        Mineral Resources   135
    Regulations and Enforcement   136
    Environment 2000—The Future   137
Transportation and Infrastructure   137
    History   137
    Administration   138
    Highways and Streets   139
    Public Transportation   140
    Railroads   140
    Aviation   140
    Waterways and Ports   141
    Financing Improvements   141

PART IV. STATE POLITICS   143

Chapter 12. Political Parties   145

What is a Party?   146
Party Enrollment   147
How Are Parties Organized?   147
    The Election District   147
    The Local Party Committee   148
    The County Committee—Base of Party Power   148
    Party Organization in New York City   149
    The State Committee   149
How the Party Chooses Its Candidates for Public Office   150
    Nomination to Statewide Office   150
Independent Nominations   151

Chapter 13. Elections—The Voters and the Candidates   153

   The Voters   153
     Who Can Vote?   154
     Who Cannot Vote?   154
     Administration of Elections   154
     Registration Procedures   156
     Types of Elections in New York State   157
     Election Day Procedures   159
     Absentee Voting   160
   The Candidates   160
     Financing Campaigns   160
     Fair Campaign Practices   162
     Judicial Campaigns   162

PART V. ACCESS TO GOVERNMENT   163

Chapter 14. Access to Government   165

   Freedom of Information Law   165
   Open Meetings Law   165
   Lobbying Regulations   167
   Ethics   167

APPENDIX: New York State Executive, Judicial, and
   Administrative Departments and Offices   169

SELECTED BIBLIOGRAPHY   173

GLOSSARY   175

INDEX   186

ABOUT THE LEAGUE OF WOMEN VOTERS OF
   NEW YORK STATE AND THE FOUNDATION
   FOR CITIZEN EDUCATION   191

LIST OF FIGURES

Figure 3-1. Judicial Departments and Districts in New York State   20

Figure 3-2. The Judiciary   21

Figure 3-3. Present Route of Appeal in the New York State Court System   22

Figure 3-4. Administration of the Courts   31

Figure 5-1. How a Bill Becomes Law   48

Figure 6-1. State Revenues (Ten Year Growth)—General Fund (Table)   59

Figure 6-2. State Revenues (Ten Year Growth)—General Fund (Graph)   61

Figure 6-3. New York State's Dollar 1987-88—General Fund   63

Figure 6-4. New York State's Dollar 1987-88—All Funds   65

Figure 6-5. Local Assistance Account 1987-88 (Disbursements)   67

Figure 7-1. A Map of New York State, Showing Counties and Principal Cities   95

Figure 9-1. School Administration on the Local Level:
   Major Types of School Districts in New York State   105

Figure 11-1. New York State Department of Environmental Conservation:
   Regions and Suboffices   127

Figure 11-2. New York State Department of Environmental Conservation:
   Organization Chart   128

Figure 11-3. Classes of Freshwater Quality   130

Figure 11-4. How a Bond Act Works   132

Figure 11-5. Regional Offices of the New York State Department of
   Transportation   139

A GUIDE TO
NEW YORK STATE
GOVERNMENT

PART I

NEW YORK STATE GOVERNMENT

CHAPTER 1
INTRODUCTION TO NEW YORK STATE

RECENT HISTORY AND TRENDS

The outstanding quality of New York State is its vitality: its diverse people, its movement, its position as the nation's financial center, its cultural life. For two expansive decades before 1975, New York lived by its motto, Excelsior! The state's policies and programs during the period gave it the nation's premier system of higher education, of support for public schools, social services and health care.

Since 1975, the direction of government has changed in basic ways. Perceptions of what state government can or should do are changing and the momentum of the past twenty years is abating. Moreover, New York has been shaken by a series of crises, among them a fiscal crisis, an energy crisis, and a crisis of confidence in government.

In the 1970s a combination of events strained state and local government resources nearly to the breaking point. The Arab oil embargo, for example, had a wrenching impact on the east coast of the United States. It undermined public confidence in the ability of government to deal with public problems and it heightened our sense of vulnerability to forces beyond our reach. At a practical level, the oil shortage increased the already high cost of power in New York and of living and doing business here.

In addition, cheaper labor in other parts of the country had been drawing manufacturing and commercial enterprise away from New York for some time. The cumulative effect of these conditions brought about a change in the state's tax policies. By the end of the 1970s, a revised tax structure increased incentives to commerce and industry in the state.

The continuing campaign to attract business is having far-reaching implications for New York's conservation programs as well. Because environmental controls that protect air and water also raise the cost of doing business, the state's conservation policies are under heavy challenge from those who argue that the use of coal and high sulfur fuels are essential to avoid a disastrous economic decline. Additionally, the siting and construction of nuclear energy facilities has encountered bitter public opposition. The state is thus at a crossroads of competing conservation and development interests.

Years of state and federal highway construction have helped business and industry reestablish themselves resulting in an increase in jobs in the suburbs. One consequence of state highway construction policies has been the loss of clientele for mass transportation and the subsequent decline of these systems. In light of the energy shortage, the state's interest in rehabilitating mass transportation is apt to pull an increasing share of state revenues for years to come.

As highway development moved industry to the suburbs, it also eroded the tax base of the central cities, incidentally enlarging their dependence on state and federal aid. The state has thus been drawn increasingly into support for local operations.

Other factors contribute even more heavily to a heightened state presence in municipal government. For twenty years New York has been developing and expanding social services to the needy, disadvantaged, and disabled, although many of the services are a shared state-local responsibility. While their cost has been doubling, tripling, and more, New York's economy has slowed and its income growth has lagged behind the growth in the cost of government.

In an effort to contain spending on social services, the state has, since 1975, changed its emphasis from seeking out those eligible for public assistance to reducing levels of eligibility, and developing cost controls. Such steps give the state an ever larger role in setting standards and policies for local government operations. At the same time, the state has not permitted the level of aid to individual recipients to rise with inflation. As a result, New York no longer heads the nation in public assistance benefits.

A major policy shift in New York's health care programs is also underway. Medicaid, for example, which brought health care within reach of large segments of the state's population, has spurred construction in both the public and private sectors of hospitals, nursing homes and other facilities. Their high cost led the state to develop a system of cost controls that has already had important consequences. One has been a plan to use the facilities more efficiently and economically, portending the closing of some and reduction of services in others. Another has been direct intervention by the state in setting standards for fees that may be charged for medical care in both the public and private sectors.

Another major development in health care and social services administration is the growth of information management systems that the state has put in place to reduce fraud, error, and overlapping services. These management controls work through cross-checking such state-kept records as withholding taxes and unemployment insurance. But the information systems also highlight the growing conflict between the state's need to protect itself against mismanagement on the one hand, and the individual's right to privacy on the other.

Policy changes in the administration of mental health programs have been particularly striking. After twenty years of building programs aimed at providing institutional care for all in need of treatment, the state has begun to dismantle its huge and relatively new mental institutions. With their enormous public authority debt still outstanding, many of the larger facilities are being phased out, not only because of their high labor and operating costs, but because concepts of treatment have changed from institutional to community based care. Moreover, drug abuse control programs, which commanded major budgetary commitments in the early 70s, have been given less priority on spending lists. Coincidentally, the agencies and courts that were organized to focus on narcotic abuse and related problems are disappearing through attrition and lack of funding.

Many cutbacks in social benefit programs reflect a political climate calling for greater austerity in government. New York State has not been threatened with "Proposition 13" (direct initiative) type restrictions, but is nevertheless responding to the pressure for limits on taxes.

One response is addressed to the property tax, the revenue mainstay of local government. Just as business taxes were eased to encourage economic growth, some changes to ease pressures on home owners are now in the air. For some time, the state has permitted partial property tax exemption for the elderly poor. The concept of the circuit breaker is also in place in legislation that offers some limited state-sponsored relief to property owners based on need.

The taxpayer movement is related to growing public emphasis on accountability in government. Spawned by the nation's experience with ethical abuses among government employees, the trend for accountability is having more than a fiscal impact. Open meetings and freedom of information laws have produced some of the more striking changes in governmental procedures. With government agencies, legislative bodies, and bureaucratic record keepers now required to open their doors and files, government is under increasing public scrutiny and pressure to develop policy in ways that the public may understand.

Accountability on a different and much larger scale followed the fiscal crisis of 1975 which closed financial markets to the City of New York, and for a period, to the state and its agencies. The city's problems and the default of one of the state's largest authorities, the Urban Development Corporation, have been responsible for a sharply increased state presence in the fiscal management of its subordinate jurisdictions. The trauma of those events have led to financial control boards in the cities, where necessary. They have also generated state controls on authority spending which has been enormously expanding government debt obligations in the past quarter century.

One of the most significant structural changes of the decade has been a far-reaching reform of the state's court system. This took shape in constitutional amendments which centralized the administration and financing of the court system; instituted new procedures for disciplining members of the judiciary; and substituted nomination and appointment of the judges of the state's highest court for the elective system. In a sense, this, too reflects the trend for accountable government.

It was predicted that by 1989 the cost of benefits paid to employees of state and local governments would exceed the three and a half billion dollar mark. How government will deal with this expense as the ratio of retirees to workers gradually increases is a major fiscal concern.

Probably the most important trend in New York State government during the 1980s was the emergence of the legislature as a coequal partner with the executive branch in the administration of state affairs, especially the budget. For instance, for Fiscal Year 1977-78 the legislature's budget was approximately $60,302,000; by Fiscal Year 1987-88 it had risen to $152,000,000. By contrast, the governor's appropriation during the same time period only increased from $6,482,523 to $8,532,843. These added funds have allowed the legislature to hire personnel and purchase hardware enabling it to challenge the executive budget previously impossible to do.

This movement toward legislative equality was also given impetus in other ways: the 1981 Court of Appeals decision in Anderson v. Regan, which stated that federal funds to the state could only be spent by legislative appropriation rather than by unilateral action on the part of the executive branch; the passage of the **Accounting, Financial Reporting and Budget Accountability Reform Act** of 1981, which, among other things strengthened the legislature's oversight of executive fiscal activities; the legislature's successful response in the Fiscal Year 1984-85 budget which reversed the governor's impoundment of certain legislatively approved funds the previous year; and the recent custom of the legislature to recess rather than adjourn after its regular session, thereby negating the governor's former power to unilaterally call the legislature into extraordinary session (see Chapter 4) and set its agenda (this trend was begun in 1975 by the adoption of a constitutional amendment giving the legislature the power to call itself into extraordinary session). Clearly the old adage of New York State government, "the Governor imposes, the Legislature disposes" has been abandoned, most likely forever.

Another change of governance in the 1980s which was felt by all levels of government throughout the country was the transfer of many responsibilities, especially in the area of public welfare, from the federal to state governments brought about by the "Reagan revolution." Other issues of the 1980s which have directly or indirectly affected New York State government were the financing of the state's infrastructure, the proper role of state and local governments in economic development, the rising cost of medical care, and governmental ethics.

A Rip Van Winkle who had napped for only five years would not recognize today's political patterns, state-local relationships or governmental procedures. The functions of state government described in the chapters that follow can be understood best in this context of change.

THE STATE CONSTITUTION

The basic law by which a democratic nation or state is governed is its constitution. In the United States we are a constitution-making people and the writing of our basic law has become symbolic of our self-government.

The Constitution of the State of New York is subordinate only to the federal constitution and statutes. Founded on the doctrine that the authority of government is derived from the people, it specifies that every provision must be approved by popular vote. Some sections have remained unchanged since their adoption in 1877 while others embody needs and convictions of succeeding generations.

State constitutions are generally much longer and more detailed than the federal constitution, which is brief, broad, and general. The more flexible nature of the federal constitution allows for redefinition and reinterpretation without amendment. Most state constitutions, on the other hand, require frequent amendment to eliminate obsolete sections and to adjust the limits of state and local powers to contemporary needs.

The New York State Constitution may be amended in two ways: either by the legislative process or by a constitutional convention. Under the first method, an amendment may be proposed in either house of the legislature. It must be passed by two successive, separately elected legislatures and submitted to the people. If it is approved by a majority of those voting on the question it becomes a part of the constitution. In the past, voters at one election have been asked to act on as many as eleven such proposals, many of a highly controversial nature.

The New York State Constitution also provides that every twenty years the question, "Shall there be a convention to revise the Constitution and amend the same?" be placed on a ballot. State voters gave a resounding "no" when that question was submitted in 1977.

The legislature may also place this question on the ballot at any other time it wishes. If the vote is favorable, delegates to a constitutional convention are chosen at the next general election. They may revise the existing constitution or write a completely new one but any change must be approved by the people.

At the time of independence, the constitution of the colony of New York was not a written document. Colonial government was based on Dutch and English customs and laws. In May 1776 the Continental Congress advised each colony to form a government of its own and write a constitution. New York's Fourth Provisional Congress was elected specifically for this purpose. Constantly in danger of capture by the British, the delegates met in White Plains, and later in Kingston. On April 20, 1777, the constitution they framed was adopted. While it embodied a profound belief in the inalienable rights of the individual, virtually all power in the state government was reserved to the landowners.

Nine conventions have been held since to revise the constitution. The convention of 1821 wrote the Bill of Rights into the basic state law. The era of Jacksonian democracy produced the constitution of 1846, which reflected expanding concepts of popular rights and government. The powers of the legislative and executive branches were curtailed, property qualifications for voting were removed, and most public offices were changed from appointive to elective.

When the 1894 convention met, corruption in government and bossism were the burning issues of the day. Distrust of public officials was coupled with the belief that the government had no part to play in the economic and social life of the times. This resulted in a constitution which, on one hand, placed severe restrictions on the legislature and, on the other, spelled out in minute detail policies intended to promote civic virtue. Among new provisions added were the merit system for civil service; limitations on the power to dispose of the state's forest preserve; and a strong state commitment to public education, public welfare and public health. This 1894 document, since amended more than 190 times, is our present constitution.

Three constitutional conventions have been held since 1894. The 1915 convention proposed 33 changes which were rejected by the voters, but many of these were later added by individual amendment. The convention of 1938 was unsuccessful in achieving its announced goal of simplifying the unduly complex document. Nevertheless it did propose new concepts of public responsibility for social welfare, including public housing and unemployment insurance, which were approved. The latest attempt to streamline this archaic document took place in 1967 when the ninth constitutional convention assembled in Albany. Its announced purpose was threefold:

• to eliminate obsolete and confusing provisions and remove unnecessary detail. (For example, specifications on the schedule of prizes that may be permitted in bingo games are still carried in New York State's Constitution.)
• to reexamine constitutional provisions requiring referenda on state bond issues and barring joint government-private undertakings
• to establish methods of legislative districting that would meet the federal **one man, one vote** standard.

Delegates to the 1967 convention were chosen on a partisan basis, and political pressures dominated the proceedings. The proposed new document was submitted to the voters as a single package in the hope that "popular" provisions would carry less popular ones. Much of the support and the opposition were then pegged to the convention's proposal to repeal the "Blaine Amendment," a section of the constitution which prohibits the state from providing aid to church related schools.

The proposed constitution was rejected by the voters in November, 1967. Some of the issues that were highly controversial then are so no longer. In the light of the U.S. Supreme Court rulings, the question of aid to parochial schools is not now a major state issue. An amendment to the federal constitution has lowered the voting age to 18. Equal population districting takes place in disregard of obsolete state constitutional standards. Fiscal issues such as the cost of the public welfare system are seen today as legislative, rather than constitutional, problems.

But even if constitutional reform no longer hangs on these questions, other basic policies are still unresolved—among them, relationships between state and local governments, financial cooperation between government and private enterprise, and limits on governmental spending. In addition, New York's charter continues to be an untidy document, filled with minutiae and exceeding 65,000 words. One Article (VII) has been amended 48 times since 1894, including nine exceptions to a single sentence prohibiting the gift or loan of state money or credit for private undertakings. The first two sentences of Article XIV, section 1, which clearly specifies that the state's forest preserve would be forever kept wild, now has approximately 880 words of exceptions to this policy. Other amendments reflect a loss of popular support for old state constitutional policies. For example, a provision forbidding gambling or wagering is followed by authorizations for bingo, parimutuel betting, and a state lottery.

Another kind of obsolescence comes not from amendments but from a continuation in the constitution of provisions that conflict with federal law. The Suffrage Article still lists qualifications for voting that have long since been superceded (see Chapter 13). The article on the legislature still contains formulas for allocating representation to the counties that were explicitly overturned by the U.S. Supreme Court in 1964.

Restrictions on raising money at both the state and local level continue to be controversial. On the one hand, New Yorkers appear to share the nationwide interest in limiting property tax increases. On the other, the legislature, with evident public support, has been looking for ways to let city school districts tax and spend beyond constitutional limits.

In another example, the constitution grants "home rule" powers which assure the ability of localities to govern themselves. However, the exercise of these powers tends to insulate local policies from the larger needs of the region or the state. The constitutional battle has intensified during the 1980s between proponents of local control and those who believe that home rule provisions interfere with the orderly management of today's economic and environmental problems.

Such limits and inconsistencies make the constitution a confusing guide to state policy. The climate of today's legislature favors measures permitting the state or local governments "to get around the constitution." The 1980s have been marked by controversial or sweeping proposed changes to the constitution which have not been enacted. The first, the proposed legalization of casino gambling in the state, was the occasion of many studies and heated debates both in the public and private sectors. During the 1979-80 legislative session, eight different amendments were approved for the first time on this issue. None passed the necessary second time, and casino gambling has since become a dormant issue. The second, a proposal to merge the state's court systems, has become the subject of much study and legislative bickering. Once again the necessary second passage failed, and the earliest that court merger could appear on the ballot is 1991.

It seems likely that the constitution will continue to suffer from an attrition of respect until in one way or another, by convention or by legislative amendment, it can accommodate to the changing needs of the state.

The state constitution consists of the following articles:

Article I: Bill of Rights
Article II: Suffrage
Article III: Legislature
Article IV: Executive
Article V: Officers and Civil Departments
Article VI: Judiciary
Article VII: State Finances
Article VIII: Local Finances
Article IX: Local Governments
Article X: Corporations
Article XI: Education
Article XII: Defense
Article XIII: Public Officers
Article XIV: Conservation
Article XV: Canals
Article XVI: Taxation
Article XVII: Social Welfare
Article XVIII: Housing
Article XIX: Amendments to Constitution
Article XX: When to Take Effect

CHAPTER 2
THE EXECUTIVE BRANCH

The Executive Branch of the government of New York State is headed by four officials who are elected by all voters of the state. In addition to the Governor, the state's most important elected official, these are the Lieutenant-Governor, the Attorney General and the Comptroller. All are elected to four year terms in even-numbered, nonpresidential years. These officials manage the many administrative departments and agencies which conduct the business of the government. Their annual salaries are set by the New York State Legislature and may be changed only by legislative action.

THE GOVERNOR

The Governor of the State of New York is the single most important official of state government. As head of the state, the governor is endowed with executive, administrative, legislative, and political powers; is constitutionally charged with implementing the laws of the state; and as chief administrator oversees all state functions. In addition to an annual salary, the governor is entitled to the use of the Executive Mansion in Albany as a residence. There is no restriction on the number of terms the governor may serve.

To qualify for the office of governor, a person must be a citizen of the United States, be at least thirty years old and a resident of New York State for at least five years prior to election.

A governor may be impeached by a majority vote of the assembly. The impeachment must then be tried by a court consisting of the Senate and the Judges of the Court of Appeals with a two-thirds majority of this court required for conviction. In the history of New York State, only one governor, William Sulzer, has been impeached and removed from office. This occurred in 1912.

Executive and Administrative Powers

The governor, as the state's chief administrator, oversees the management of all state departments and agencies. With the advice and consent of the Senate, the governor appoints the heads of most departments, boards and commissions and may also remove them from office.

Three major department heads are not appointed by the governor. The attorney general, who heads the Department of Law, and the comptroller, who heads the Department of Audit and Control, are both elected by the people. The head of the Department of Education is appointed by the Regents of the University of the State of New York.

Even with these exceptions to the governor's appointive powers, the prerogative to examine and investigate the management and affairs of any department, board, agency, or commission contributes greatly to the control of state administration.

The governor's role in budget making is another key factor in shaping the administration because the state's budget, which is prepared by the Division of the Budget, reflects the policies and programs of the governor. Additionally, the expenditure plans of all departments must be approved by the governor.

To some extent, the governor also plays a role in the Judicial Branch of the government by appointing judges of the Court of Appeals and the Court of Claims with the advice and consent of the Senate. The governor also designates who will serve in the four Appellate Divisions of the Court and fills vacancies on the Supreme Court, Surrogate's Court, County Court, Family Court (outside New York City), and District Court.

In cases of unusual or highly sensitive crimes, when it is considered that the local prosecutor's efforts will be hampered in providing a fair trial, or when residents of a community are convinced that the prosecution will be biased, the governor may appoint a special prosecutor to handle the case.

The power of pardon is another quasijudicial function of the governor. Except in cases of treason and impeachment, the governor may grant reprieves, commutations, and pardons after conviction. Even in cases of treason, the governor may suspend execution of sentence until the next meeting of the legislature, at which time the legislature assumes jurisdiction.

The governor also is empowered to appoint special commissions of investigation, known as Moreland Act Commissions, to inquire into the conduct in office of any public officer or body; any matter concerning the execution or enforcement of state laws; and any matter concerning public peace, public safety and public justice. In addition, the governor may remove certain locally elected officials, including district attorneys and sheriffs, for misconduct in office.

As Commander-in-Chief of the New York State National Guard, the governor appoints its head and, with the consent of the Senate, all major-generals, all of whom must be federally qualified. The governor, using discretionary powers, assigns units of the guard to deal with emergencies that arise in any part of the state.

To a large degree, the governor's administrative functions are exercised by staff members in the Executive Department. Some of the important members of the governor's staff are the secretary, counsel, budget director and communications director.

Legislative Powers

Because programs and policies heavily influence the agenda of each legislative session, the governor is often called the state's chief legislator. Although the governor may not introduce bills to the legislature, a legislative program, in the form of a large number of administration bills, may be introduced by individual legislators. Usually, the bills are introduced through legislative leaders or through chairmen of the committees concerned with the particular legislation. In this way, the governor's measures are assured a hearing.

The governor is required to report to the legislature at the beginning of each session in a "State of the State" message which outlines the state government's past accomplishments and the governor's future goals. The governor also must submit to the legislature an executive budget and supporting revenue proposals.

Limitations on the Governor's Powers

Although the governor's authority is extensive, it does have limitations. The governor cannot spend any public money except as authorized by the legislature. A veto of legislation may be overridden by a two-thirds vote in each house of the legislature. The governor shares a measure of responsibility with the comptroller and attorney general, but has little authority or control over them. Although the governor has the right to propose programs, they cannot be enacted without legislative approval. Finally, the need to obtain the consent of the Senate in many cases of appointments, and the existence of boards with long-term members who may have been appointed by a previous governor, substantially limits the governor's powers of appointment as well as control of policy-making boards.

Political Role of the Governor

The governor's influence is extended through the role as titular leader of a political party. From the time of nomination as a candidate for the office, the governor, whose positions are normally reflected in the party's platform, acquires great political prestige. After election, high political standing helps the governor to shape legislation intended to carry out the party platform. The governor is naturally better able to see policies and programs adopted if the party also succeeds in electing a majority of the members of the legislature. The governor's ability to command public attention helps mobilize public opinion and focus it on legislative objectives.

In sum, the governor's effectiveness is enhanced by a research staff; by the information available through the administrative departments; by the part-time nature of the legislature as compared to the governor's full-time postition; by the role of party leader; and by the high visibility of the office.

THE LIEUTENANT-GOVERNOR

The lieutenant-governor is elected on a joint ballot with the governor to insure that both will be of the same party. The constitution envisions the office of lieutenant-governor as a stand-by office to insure orderly succession should the governor be unable to serve for any reason. Qualifications for the lieutenant-governor are the same as those for the governor. Should the lieutenant-governor, for any reason, succeed to the office of governor, no election would be held to fill the office of lieutenant-governor for the balance of the term.

Other than acting in the absence of the governor, the only specific duty assigned to the lieutenant-governor by the constitution is to serve as presiding officer of the Senate.

THE ATTORNEY GENERAL

As head of the Department of Law, the attorney general is the state's chief legal officer and provides legal services to departments and agencies of state government. In addition to civil responsibilities in these areas, the attorney general prosecutes criminal violations of the Labor, Workers Compensation, Unemployment, Insurance, Conservation and Tax Laws.

Additionally, the attorney general also prosecutes fraudulent sales of stocks and securities and violations of the General Business Law and is perhaps most widely known to the public for his ability to prosecute frauds against consumers.

The Statewide Organized Crime Task Force is based in the attorney general's office. Its function is to investigate and prosecute organized crime activities which cross county lines and to assist, or, if necessary, supplant county district attorneys in that effort.

As the state's chief attorney, the attorney general frequently serves as an advisor when there are questions about the constitutionality of bills and legislative acts.

THE COMPTROLLER

The comptroller is the chief fiscal officer of the state and heads the Department of Audit and Control and directs all of its activities relating to cash management, state debt and investment. This department audits the accounts and records of all state agencies and supervises the affairs of more than 9000 local governments, school districts and other quasigovernmental bodies. The comptroller also administers the state retirement systems and the New York State Social Security Agency and is custodian of their funds.

VACANCIES

In case of vacancy in the offices of both governor and lieutenant-governor, a governor and a lieutenant-governor shall be elected for the remainder of the term at the next general election happening not less than three months after both offices become vacant.

In case of vacancy in the offices of both governor and lieutenant-governor, or if both are impeached, absent from the state or otherwise unable to serve, the Temporary President of the Senate shall serve as governor until the inabilities have ceased or until a governor is elected.

If the Temporary President of the Senate, while acting as governor, is away from the state, is unable to serve for any reason, or if that office becomes vacant, the Speaker of the Assembly shall act as governor.

CHAPTER 3
THE JUDICIAL BRANCH

In the Judicial Branch of the state government, all courts in New York, except the federal courts, are part of the state's unified court system. Although the state constitution defines in general terms the powers and duties of each court, it also gives the Legislature limited power to determine the kinds of matters a particular court may consider. In addition, the constitution gives the legislature the power to establish and discontinue some lower courts. The constitution also sets judicial qualifications and provides for the selection and removal of judges.

New York State has one of the most intricate court systems in the nation. It is divided geographically into four Judicial Departments, each with its own intermediate appeals court which is known as the Appellate Division of the Supreme Court. Each judicial department is divided into judicial districts which are composed of one or more counties. A supreme court is located in each judicial district. Altogether, the state has 12 judicial districts; half of these are located in the most heavily populated part of the state, the New York City metropolitan area (see Figure 3-1).

COURT STRUCTURE AND JURISDICTION

There are two fundamental types of courts: original, or trial courts, where cases begin; and appellate courts, which hear appeals from the decisions of other courts. There are eleven different trial courts within the state system (see Figure 3-2).

Appellate Courts

THE COURT OF APPEALS

The Court of Appeals is the highest court in the state and is located in Albany. In state government, it is the equivalent of the United States Supreme Court. Generally, this court reviews questions of law. Individuals or groups may appeal directly from a trial court to the Court of Appeals if the question involved is restricted to constitutionality of either a state or federal statute.

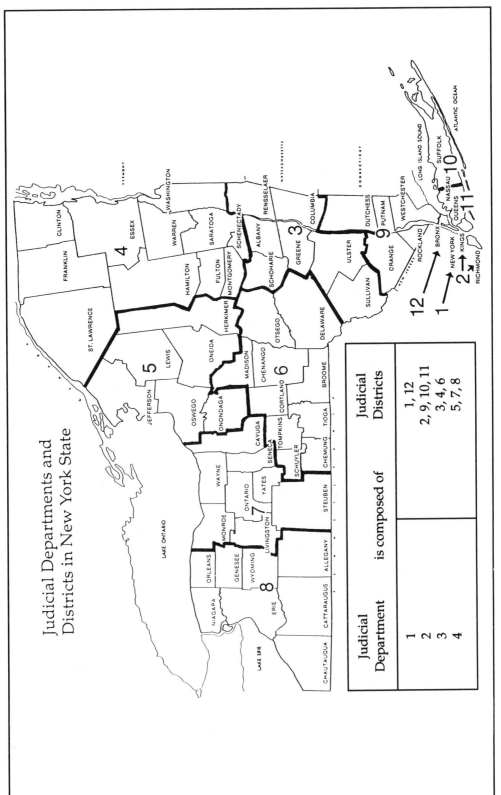

Judicial Departments and Districts in New York State

Judicial Department	is composed of	Judicial Districts
1		1, 12
2		2, 9, 10, 11
3		3, 4, 6
4		5, 7, 8

Figure 3-1

The remainder of the calendar is controlled by the court and consists of hearing selected appeals from the Appellate Division. The court's decisions are final and can only be appealed to the United States Supreme Court in cases involving federal constitutional questions. The Court of Appeals is also responsible for determining policy for the administration of the state's court system.

The Court of Appeals consists of the Chief Judge and six Associate Judges. Five members of the court constitute a quorum, and concurrence (agreement) by four members is required for a decision.

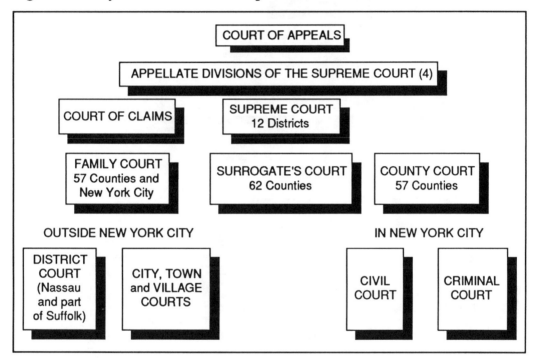

Figure 3-2: **The Judiciary**

THE APPELLATE DIVISIONS
The appellate division in each judicial department is the first level of appeals from four trial courts: Supreme, Family, Surrogate's, and Claims. The responsibilities of the appellate divisions include resolving appeals from the trial courts in civil and criminal cases and conducting proceedings to admit, suspend, or disbar lawyers. Up to five justices may hear each case, but three must agree for a decision.

APPELLATE TERMS OF THE SUPREME COURT

An appellate division may establish an Appellate Term to ease the division's case load. Appellate Terms have been established in large downstate urban and suburban areas in the First and Second Judicial Departments (see Figure 3-3). The Appellate Term hears civil and criminal appeals from local courts and certain appeals from county courts. An Appellate Term consists of three to five Supreme Court justices. At least two justices must hear an appeal and concur in a decision.

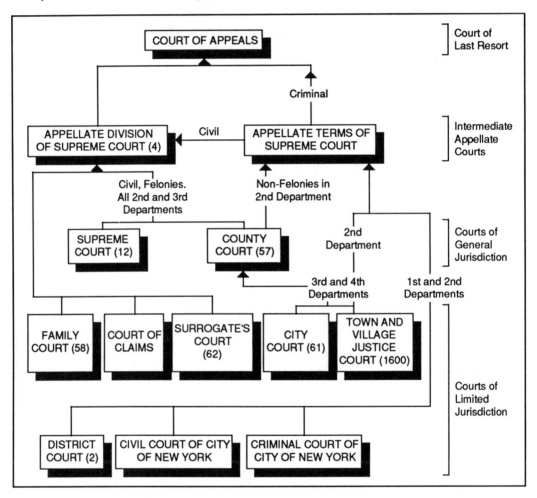

Figure 3-3: **Present Route of Appeal in the New York State Court System**

COUNTY COURTS

In the Third and Fourth Judicial Departments, which have no Appellate Terms, the county courts hear appeals from the local city, town, and village courts. Appeals from the county courts generally go to the Appellate Division of the Supreme Court.

Trial Courts (Courts of Original Jurisdiction)

THE SUPREME COURT

The New York State Supreme Court is a court of original jurisdiction, which means that cases begin in that court. Although any type of case may begin in the Supreme Court, this court usually hears cases that are outside the jurisdiction of the specialized courts. In general, Supreme Court cases involve: civil matters dealing with monetary amounts above the jurisdiction of lower courts (e.g., negligence cases); divorce, separation, and annulment proceedings; and equity suits (e.g., mortgage foreclosures). In some large metropolitan areas, including New York City, the Supreme Court also hears felony prosecutions.

Supreme Court decisions may be appealed to a higher court, either in an Appellate Division of the state's Supreme Court or the Court of Appeals, or both.

THE COUNTY COURT

Every county outside of New York City has a county court. County courts handle criminal prosecutions, mostly for crimes that carry prison sentences of one year or more incarceration (felony). They also handle civil cases which involve monetary amounts up to $25,000.

THE FAMILY COURT

Every county, including the five counties of New York City combined as one, has a Family Court. This court handles many types of family problems, including:

- juvenile delinquency
- child protection, abuse, and neglect
- persons in need of supervision, or PINS (males under 16 and females under 18 who are ungovernable or beyond the control of parents)
- review and approval of foster-care placements
- paternity determinations
- family offenses
- adoptions (concurrent jurisdiction with Surrogate's Court)
- support of dependent relatives
- spouse abuse (a felony, and may be tried either in a criminal court or in Family Court).

Family Court does not handle cases involving divorce, separation, annulment proceedings, or, except on referral from Supreme Court, title to marital property.

Appeals from the Family Court go to the Appellate Division of the Supreme Court.

THE SURROGATE'S COURT

Every county in the state has a Surrogate's Court to hear cases involving the affairs of deceased persons, such as the probate of wills and the administration of estates. Surrogate's Court shares concurrent jurisdiction with Family Court over adoptions. Appeals from the Surrogate's Court go to the Appellate Division of the Supreme Court.

THE COURT OF CLAIMS

The Court of Claims is a special trial court which is limited to trying claims against the State of New York. The court has headquarters in Albany and sits in various locations across the state. Appeals from the Court of Claims go to the Appellate Division of the Supreme Court.

Local Trial Courts (Courts of Original Jurisdiction)

Local courts outside New York City fall into four categories: district, city, town, and village courts.

THE DISTRICT COURT

A district court is created after a request by a local government(s) and approval of the voters in that area. Any county, except those in New York City, or any portion of a county consisting of contiguous towns/cities may request a district court as a local option. District court jurisdiction extends to civil cases involving up to $15,000 and to criminal cases involving misdemeanors, violations, and offenses.

The state has only two District Courts, both in the Second Judicial Department. One is in Nassau County and the other in the western part of Suffolk County. District Court appeals generally are heard by the Appellate Term of the Supreme Court.

TOWN AND VILLAGE COURTS

The jurisdiction of the town and village courts in **criminal cases** includes **misdemeanors** and lesser offenses: violations, which carry penalties of not more than 15 days in jail; misdemeanors, which carry penalties of 15 days to one year. Town and village courts can hear civil cases involving amounts up to $3000.

The judges of these courts have the power to issue warrants for the arrest of people charged with crimes. The judges hold **preliminary hearings** and **arraignments** for those charged with more serious crimes and determine whether or not the accused should be released on their own recognizance, released on bail, or detained pending **grand jury** action. Appeals generally go to the county courts in the 3rd and 4th Judicial Departments and to the Appellate Term of the Supreme Court in the 2nd Judicial Department.

CITY COURTS OUTSIDE NEW YORK CITY

City courts exist in 61 cities and have criminal jurisdiction over misdemeanors and lesser offenses. Their civil jurisdiction was standardized in 1988 to a maximum of $15,000 to be phased in over a three-year period. Some city courts have a small claims part for informal disposition of matters not exceeding $2000 and/or a housing part for hearing housing violations and landlord/tenant disputes. The judges of these courts are empowered to issue warrants of arrest. Appeals generally go to the county courts in the 3rd and 4th Judicial Departments and to the Appellate Term of the Supreme Court in the 2nd Judicial Department.

New York City Courts

A. The Civil Court of the City of New York tries civil cases involving amounts up to $25,000. It also includes a small claims part with a $2000 limit, and a housing part.

B. The Criminal Court of the City of New York conducts trials of misdemeanors and violations. Criminal Court judges also act as magistrates, as do city, town, and village judges outside New York City.

Appeals go to the Appellate Term of the Supreme Court.

JUDICIAL SELECTION

The state constitution mandates the methods for selecting judges. Some judges are elected and some are appointed, and the issue of an appointive versus an elective judiciary has been controversial throughout the state's history.

In the state's early history, judges were appointed by a Council of Appointment. In 1821, the council was abolished and the governor received power to appoint all judges with Senate confirmation. However, in 1846, New Yorkers, responding to the philosophy of Jacksonian democracy and weary of abuses stemming from landowners' control of the judiciary, abolished the system of appointed judges and established a completely elective judiciary. By 1894, boss control of nominations and elections prompted a partial return to the appointive system. The governor was given the power to appoint justices of the Appellate Division of the Supreme Court, and the mayor of New York City was given authority to appoint Criminal Court Judges. In 1949, the governor's appointive power was extended to the appointment, with Senate confirmation, of judges to the newly created Court of Claims. In 1962, the mayor of New York City was given the power to appoint judges of the Family Court in that city. Finally, a constitutional amendment approved in 1977 established a **merit selection system** for the governor's appointments of judges to the Court of Appeals.

Judges of the Supreme Court, County Court, Surrogate's Court, Family Court (except in New York City), New York City Civil Court, District Court, and town courts are all elected by popular vote. With confirmation by the Senate, the governor appoints judges for the Court of Claims and fills vacancies on the Supreme, County, Surrogate's, and Family Courts until the next general election. Although currently in use, screening panels for appointments are not mandated by the constitution. Screening panels review qualifications and recommend candidates for judicial appointment.

Qualifications and Terms of Office

Judges and justices in New York State come to the bench in a variety of ways, depending on the court of service, and are subject to a variety of qualification requirements, lengths of service, and salaries.

JUDGES OF THE COURT OF APPEALS

The judges of the state's top court are appointed by the governor from candidates recommended by the Commission on Judicial Nomination. The appointments must be approved by the state Senate. The Commission on Judicial Nomination consists of 12 members serving four-year staggered terms. Four of its members are appointed by the governor, four by the Chief Judge of the Court of Appeals, and one each by the Speaker of the Assembly, the Temporary President of the Senate (Majority Leader), and the two legislative minority leaders. No more than six may be of the same political party, at least four (two each of the governor's and the Chief Judge's appointees) must not be lawyers, and none may be active judges. None may hold office in any political party, and all must be residents of the state.

The Commission on Judicial Nomination must be notified by the clerk of the Court of Appeals no later than eight months before a vacancy is to occur, or immediately in cases of death or resignation.

Two weeks before the vacancy, the Commission must submit to the governor the names of seven people it considers well qualified for the position of Chief Judge. For the position of Associate Judge, it submits three to seven names. The governor makes the appointment from the names submitted, no sooner than fifteen days and no later than thirty days after receiving them.

All of the commission's proceedings and records are confidential; only the governor has access to all of its information on the candidates recommended. The commission's final report is made public. Although all candidates must submit financial statements, only the financial statement of the person actually appointed is made public. Court of Appeals judges serve fourteen-year terms.

APPELLATE DIVISION JUSTICES

Supreme Court Justices are appointed to the Appellate Divisions by the governor. The governor also appoints a chief justice, called the Presiding Justice, in each division. The four presiding justices, with the Chief Judge of the Court of Appeals, constitute the **Administrative Board**.

Presiding justices serve for the duration of their Supreme Court terms. The associate appellate justices serve for five years or for the remainder of their terms, whichever is shorter.

There are 24 appellate justice positions authorized by law but if an appellate division certifies a need, the governor can appoint additional justices. There are presently 13 appellate justices serving in the First Judicial Department, 15 in the Second, nine in the Third and ten in the Fourth, a total of 47 Appellate Justices.

SUPREME COURT JUSTICES

Supreme Court justices are elected by the voters in the judicial district in which they serve. Candidates are nominated by Judicial District Conventions held by each political party, usually in middle to late September of a year in which a Supreme Court post will become vacant. Sometimes the parties will cross-endorse the same candidate, so the same name appears on two or more party lines on the ballot. Cross-endorsed candidates frequently have no opposition.

Supreme Court justices must have been members of the bar for at least ten years. They serve fourteen-year terms or until age 70, whichever comes first.

COUNTY COURT JUDGES

County Court judges are elected by the voters in the county in which they serve after nomination by the county political parties. They must have been members of the bar for five years and residents of their county. They serve ten-year terms.

FAMILY COURT JUDGES

Family Court judges outside of New York City are elected by the voters of the county. They are nominated by the same process as County Court judges and must have been members of the bar for ten years. They serve ten-year terms.

In New York City, Family Court judges are appointed by the mayor for ten-year terms.

SURROGATE'S COURT JUDGES

Surrogate's Court judges are also elected by the voters of the county in which they serve and are nominated in the same manner as County and Family Court judges. They serve fourteen-year terms in New York City and ten-year terms elsewhere. They must have been members of the bar for ten years.

COURT OF CLAIMS JUDGES

The governor appoints, with Senate confirmation, judges to the Court of Claims for nine-year terms. Each must have been a member of the bar for at least ten years.

DISTRICT COURT JUDGES

District Court judges are elected by the voters in their districts following nomination by county political parties. They must be residents of their districts and members of the bar for at least five years. District Court judges serve six-year terms.

TOWN AND VILLAGE COURT JUSTICES

Town and village courts are the only courts that do not require justices to be members of the bar. Of approximately 2400 town and village court justices in New York State, about 2000 are not lawyers. Nonlawyers must take and pass an initial examination administered by the Office of Court Administration as well as attend an annual advanced course. Lawyers are required to attend annual advanced courses. Town and village justices are elected for four-year terms.

CITY COURT JUDGES OUTSIDE NEW YORK CITY

City Court judges are either elected by the voters or appointed by local authorities. They must have been members of the bar for at least five years. Full-time judges serve ten-year terms; part-time judges serve six-year terms.

NEW YORK CITY CIVIL COURT JUDGES

Civil Court judges in New York City are elected for ten-year terms. They must have been members of the bar for at least ten years.

Criminal Court judges are appointed by the mayor of New York City for ten-year terms. They must have been members of the bar for at least ten years.

Retirement of Judges and Justices

The state constitution requires that all state judges retire at age 70, except for Court of Appeals judges and Supreme Court justices who can serve on the Supreme Court and the Appellate Division up to six additional years if certified as physically and mentally fit.

However, since a 1987 amendment to the **Federal Age Discrimination In Employment Act** eliminated mandatory retirement for all appointed officials, state judges who are appointed may remain in office after the age of 70 to completion of their terms despite the state constitutional restriction. Elected state judges remain subject to the constitutionally mandated retirement age of 70 years.

COURT ADMINISTRATION

The state's court system is administered by the Chief Administrator, who is appointed by the Chief Judge of the Court of Appeals with the advice and consent of the Administrative Board. (If the Chief Administrator is a judge, the title of the office is Chief Administrative Judge.) On behalf of the Chief Judge, the Chief Administrator prepares the annual budgets of all courts of the unified court system, except for town and village courts; establishes terms of court and assigns judges to them; and generally regulates the flow of business in the courts by court practice rules (see Figure 3-4).

The Chief Administrator also is charged with hiring and supervising personnel; labor relations and collective bargaining with nonjudicial court employees; gathering and reporting statistical data; preparing legislative proposals to improve the efficiency of the courts; setting up continuing education programs for judges and court employees; and planning and developing court improvement projects.

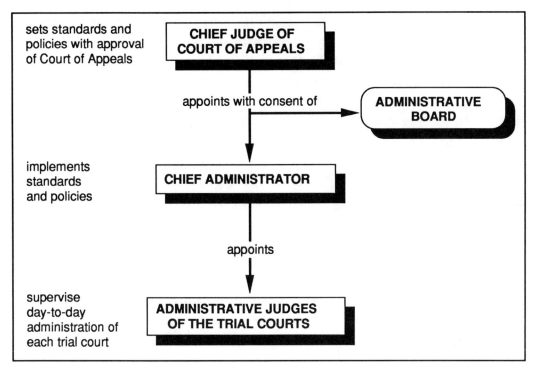

Figure 3-4: **Administration of the Courts**

The Chief Administrator's staff includes administrative judges in the various counties and judicial districts of the state, serving out of regional staff offices. The Chief Judge and the Chief Administrator are legally required to consult with the Administrative Board of the Courts and with the Judicial Conference.

The Administrative Board is composed of the Chief Judge of the Court of Appeals and the four presiding justices of the appellate divisions. The Judicial Conference is composed of judges who represent each of the trial courts and practicing lawyers from various parts of the state.

FINANCING THE COURTS

In 1976, the legislature adopted a **Unified Court Budget Act** which merged 120 separate court budgets into the state's judicial budget. The state also assumed responsibility for the operating costs of the courts over a four-year period except for town and village courts. By 1980, the state had assumed total funding of all operating costs of the courts except for the town and village courts which continue to be funded by their respective local governments.

While the state assumes responsibility for the operating costs of the courts, repair and maintenance of courthouses remain the responsibility of local governments. Statewide, court facilities have been deteriorating for many years because local funds were not committed for rehabilitation of the physical structures. In 1987, the legislature passed the court facilities bill to help local governments finance courthouse improvements. The New York State Dormitory Authority is authorized to issue up to $1.25 billion in bonds for courthouse construction and repair; a state fund, financed by increases in court user fees, will reimburse a percentage of the interest on the loans for courthouse improvements and for the cost of maintaining the court facilities.

JUDICIAL DISCIPLINE

The New York State Commission on Judicial Conduct is the disciplinary agency designated by the constitution to review complaints of misconduct against judges of the state's unified court system.

The commission consists of eleven members who serve four-year staggered terms. Four are appointed by the governor, three by the Chief Judge of the Court of Appeals, and one each by the four leaders of the legislature. The constitution requires four members to be judges, at least one an attorney, and at least two nonlawyers. The commission elects one of its members as chairperson and appoints an administrator and a clerk who are in charge of day-to-day operations.

The types of complaints that may be investigated by the commission include: improper demeanor, conflicts of interest, intoxication, bias, prejudice, favoritism, gross neglect, corruption, certain prohibited political activity, and other misconduct on or off the bench.

Role of the Commission

The commission receives and reviews written complaints of misconduct against judges, initiates complaints, conducts formal hearings, subpoenas witnesses and documents, and makes determinations to dismiss or discipline. The commission does not make decisions related to judicial rulings of judges. Those decisions go through the appellate process. The commission is not expected to expose crimes, nor does it have the traditional powers of a prosecuting agency. After investigating and conducting a hearing, the commission may admonish, censure, remove a judge from office or retire a judge for disability. The commission can also issue private, informal reprimands to deal with minor instances of judicial misbehavior.All of the commission's proceedings are confidential through the conclusion of the hearing. If the commission finds cause for disciplinary action against a judge, its findings are made available to the public through the office of the clerk of the Court of Appeals. The commission also publishes an annual report which is available to the public. Decisions of the commission may be appealed to the Court of Appeals, which can uphold, dismiss, reduce, or upgrade the disciplinary action. The commission is independent of the unified court system, and is funded by the state legislature.

ATTORNEYS

Lawyers have special responsibilities in the administration of justice which are to represent the interest of their client, to present evidence favorable to the client and to enable the judge or the jury to reach a just decision. The lawyer safeguards the client's rights and interests throughout all phases of a trial.

Their admission to practice is carefully supervised. The New York State Board of Law Examiners, consisting of three lawyers appointed by the Court of Appeals, holds examinations twice each year for admission of attorneys. The names of those passing these tests are certified to the appellate divisions, which inquire into the character and fitness of candidates residing in their respective departments. Applicants are sworn in as attorneys and counsellors-at-law only after all of these requirements are satisfied. Attorneys guilty of serious misconduct may be disbarred or temporarily suspended from practice by the appellate divisions.

All attorneys licensed to practice law in New York State are bound by the provisions of the Lawyer's Code of Professional Responsibility. Violations of the code can result in a range of disciplinary measures from a letter of caution to disbarment. There is a disciplinary panel that operates under the supervision of the Appellate Divisions of the State Supreme Court in each of the four judicial departments, or regions.

Counsel for the Indigent

By state law, the accused has the right to counsel at all stages of a criminal proceeding. If the accused is charged with a misdemeanor or felony and cannot afford counsel, the court must provide an attorney if the defendant requests one. In most cases, the judge decides whether or not the accused is entitled to free counsel. Sources of court-provided counsel include public defenders, private legal aid societies, and assigned counsel.

In civil matters, all parties in most Family Court proceedings, including children, have the right to an attorney. The court will usually assign a lawyer to a party who cannot afford one. Legal assistance also is provided in child support cases for both parents. Many agencies and programs provide civil legal representation for the poor.

THE JURY

Juries are an integral part of the due process of law in our courts. The jury system has also been called the "community arm of the courts" because it is the principal, and sometimes the only, contact citizens have with the courts. There are two kinds of juries in every county: the **grand jury** and the **trial jury**, which is sometimes called the petit jury.

The grand jury, composed of 16 to 23 people, is drawn from the same county jury pool as the trial jury. At least 16 jurors must be present at each meeting and the agreement of 12 jurors is necessary to return an indictment.The grand jury has two functions, the indicting function and the investigative function. In its indicting function the grand jury holds hearings and takes sworn testimony to determine if there is legally sufficient evidence to indict, that is, to hold for trial a person accused of a serious crime (felony, a crime punishable by a prison term of a year or more). If the grand jury finds the evidence insufficient, it can hand down a "no true bill." If it finds that a person should be prosecuted for lesser charges, it may direct the district attorney to do so.

The constitution guarantees that all people accused of felonies are entitled to grand jury hearings. The basis for this right is the belief that no one should be sent to trial unless there is some substantial foundation for the charge, as well as the belief that the grand jury hearing is the appropriate vehicle for screening these charges. Defendants accused of less than a Class A felony (punishable by 15 years to life incarceration) may waive the right to a grand jury hearing if the district attorney agrees, if the court is satisfied the waiver has been executed properly, and if a grand jury indictment has not already been handed down.

The **district attorney** is the sole legal adviser to the grand jury and subpoenas witnesses in the name of the grand jury. The grand jury may conduct investigations and bring indictments on its own initiative, but the more usual course is for the district attorney to present the evidence and request that an indictment be returned. Generally, the only evidence the grand jury hears is the case for the prosecution. The defense will be presented at the actual trial if an indictment is handed down. A grand jury never determines whether a person is, in fact, guilty. That is the function of the trial jury.

Witnesses appearing before the grand jury are automatically granted immunity from prosecution on any charges concerning the matter about which testimony is given. They are not entitled to counsel unless they waive this immunity. If a witness signs a waiver of immunity in front of the grand jury, he/she is entitled to counsel in an advisory capacity only.

All grand jury proceedings are held in secret. The only people present are the jurors, the district attorney, an administrative clerk, a stenographer, an interpreter (if necessary), the witness who is testifying, and, in certain cases, the attorney for the witness before it. The primary purpose of secret proceedings is to protect the witness from intimidation or harassment.

The other function of the grand jury is to conduct investigations concerning the conduct, malfeasance, or neglect in public office by a public servant, whether criminal or not. Grand juries also may inquire into prison conditions.

Trial Juries—Civil and Criminal

Trial juries hear sworn testimony and decide questions of fact during a trial. A civil trial is a means of resolving a dispute between two parties. A broad range of subjects is covered by the civil law including injury to person or property, breach of contract, contested divorce, and validity of wills. Six-person juries decide civil cases, with agreement of five necessary for a verdict or judgment.

In criminal cases, individuals are prosecuted by the government, in the name of the people, for violating statutes which define particular crimes. The function of the jury is to decide if the facts are sufficient to establish guilt beyond a reasonable doubt.

Crimes are divided into two categories: **felonies**, which carry a prison term of more than one year and **misdemeanors**, which carry a maximum sentence of one year. Crimes are further subdivided into degrees of seriousness. In felony cases, defendants are entitled to a jury of twelve persons, in misdemeanor cases, a jury of six persons. A unanimous verdict is necessary to convict a person of a crime.

The right to a trial by jury exists in most but not all types of cases. A right to trial by jury may be waived by the parties in a civil case or by the defendant in a criminal case, except for murder in the first degree.

Article 16 of the Judiciary Law lists qualifications, exemptions and disqualifications for jury service. These are the same for trial jurors and grand jurors.

Qualifications: In order to qualify as a juror a person must:

1. Be a citizen of the United States and a resident of the county
2. Be not less than eighteen years of age (A 1987 law removed the requirement that a juror must be less than 76 years of age)
3. Not have a mental or physical condition which causes the person to be incapable of performing in a reasonable manner the duties of a juror
4. Not have been convicted of a felony
5. Be intelligent, of good character, able to read and write the English language with a degree of proficiency sufficient to fill out satisfactorily the juror qualification questionnaire, and be able to speak the English language in an understandable manner. (Note: Deaf and blind persons are not automatically excluded from jury duty).

Disqualifications: Each of the following is disqualified from serving as a juror:

1. Members in active service in the armed forces of the United States
2. Elected federal, state, city, county, town, or village officers
3. The head of a civil department of the federal, state, city, county, town or village government; a member of a public authority or state commission or board; secretary to the governor
4. A federal judge or magistrate or a judge of the unified court system
5. A person who has served on a grand or petit jury within the state, including in a federal court, within two years of the date of the next proposed service.

Although jury service is the civic responsibility of all qualified citizens, 28 occupational classes are currently exempt or disqualified from jury duty.

The Office of Court Administration has the ultimate responsibility for jury management. Each county has a commissioner of jurors, paid from the judiciary budget, who oversees the process of summoning and qualifying jurors. The commissioners also ensure that the courts in each county have an adequate number of qualified jurors who represent a cross-section of the population.

A computer system in the Office of Court Administration provides all 62 counties with lists of potential jurors. This computer-generated jury-call method combines three source lists into a single master list for each county, eliminates duplicate names, then randomly selects names of prospective jurors. The source lists include the names of those filing income tax returns, licensed drivers and registered voters. Persons may also volunteer to serve as jurors. Both grand and trial jurors are selected at random from the same master list of qualified jurors in each county.

State law permits Commissioners of Jurors, or the trial court, to excuse or postpone jury service to a future date of service if the date of summoning causes undue hardship or extreme inconvenience to the person called, a person under his/her care, or to the public. Approximately one million jury service summonses are sent out in New York State each year and half result in postponement requests which are usually granted.

Juror Fees

Legislation passed in 1988, effective in April 1989, provides for a uniform statewide juror fee of $15 per day and an additional $6 per day for every day of attendance at a trial lasting more than 30 days. Prior to passage of this legislation, juror service fees ranged from $1 to $15 per day, depending on the county. The juror fee is intended to help defray expenses incurred by jurors while fulfilling their civic duty, not to compensate for the work done.

Enforcement

Failure to respond to the juror qualification questionnaires and to jury summonses has been an increasingly serious problem in New York State. Nonresponse to the summonses is as high as 67 percent in some counties. Those who fail to respond can be fined up to $250 but this penalty can be imposed only after notice to the person called and a hearing before the court or a judicial hearing officer.

CHAPTER 4
THE LEGISLATIVE BRANCH

The New York State Legislature is older than the U.S. Congress. Established as a lawmaking body in 1777 under the state's first constitution, it met first at Kingston before settling in Albany. Its size and composition have been altered repeatedly over the years, but it has remained a bicameral body whose two houses—the Senate and the Assembly—have coequal powers.

After each federal census, the legislature remaps its own districts, 150 in the Assembly and a number in the Senate that may vary upward from 50. For the past several years there have been 61 Senate districts. Today these districts are based almost exclusively on equal population standards. Other directives for districting long in need of amendment remain imbedded in the state constitution although they were largely superceded by the U.S. Supreme Court's one man, one vote decision more than 25 years ago.

POWERS AND LIMITATIONS OF THE LEGISLATURE

The New York State Legislature has the power to make laws in all areas except those which have been reserved to the federal government or to the people. It may adopt programs affecting public health, safety and welfare; raise revenues; regulate business; create and abolish political subdivisions, grant them powers and regulate their operations. It may establish its own districts and those from which members of congress are elected. It may confirm, remove and impeach public officials and propose amendments to the state and federal constitutions.

This broad authority however, is subject to some limits. Both the federal and state constitutions prohibit legislation which infringes on individual rights and liberties. The Home Rule Article, through provisions designed to protect local self-government, bars the legislature from passing laws which apply only to a single locality unless expressly requested to do so by the governing body of that community. Nor can the legislature pass private or local bills changing the names of persons or locating or changing a county seat. The detailed nature of the state constitution places substantial limits as well on the legislature's freedom to act in important areas of governmental concern, such as the raising and spending of public money and providing for public housing.

One may view the legislature as a mediator in the conflicts among various interest groups within the state. It defines the state's priorities through the programs it enacts. Its tax laws determine how fiscal burdens of these programs shall be shared by the public and private sectors. Its appropriation decisions expanding or limiting programs in operation reflect public reaction to state programs and policies.

The legislative process is complicated by political factors in other ways. With the two houses frequently divided between the two parties, the minority in one house can generally count on its party majority in the other chamber to block action on major partisan issues. Impasses of this sort may hold up adjournment, may require the governor's intervention in working out a compromise, or may totally obstruct progress on a controversial matter.

As an independent branch of the state government, the legislature has the authority to make rules for its own proceedings, choose its own officers and judge the election and qualifications of its own members. In order to permit the public to follow its deliberations, legislative sessions are open; and free debate is guaranteed by its rules. Statements made in the course of debate are "privileged," and may not form the basis of a libel suit or prosecution in any other tribunal.

THE LEGISLATORS

The men and women who exercise these broad legislative powers may come from any walk of life and represent any vocation or profession. For much of this century, lawyers dominated legislative ranks. Legislators are technically part-time officials who may carry on private business or professions in addition to their legislative duties, but about one-third now list no other occupation but legislator. Many others give nearly full time to the demanding cycle of legislative business, constituent concerns, and campaign politics.

Terms for both senators and members of the Assembly are two years, but most legislators seek reelection. Some stay in office for as long as 30 years. A member's length of service may be a factor in committee assignment, appointment to chairmanships and general effectiveness.

Members of the legislature must be citizens of the United States, residents of New York State for five years, and of their Assembly or Senate District for one year prior to their election. While serving in the legislature, they may not hold any other elective office, except as a delegate to a constitutional convention; nor may they be appointed to any office which was either created or had its salary increased during their legislative term.

Legislative salaries are fixed by law. The political difficulty of raising their own salaries led the lawmakers to adopt a measure in 1979 authorizing periodic future increases. Their salaries were $32,960 in 1983 and for 1989 were raised to $57,500. In 1988 the per diem expenses budgeted for both houses totaled over $3,200,000.

Legislative leaders, committee chairmen, and ranking minority members of committees receive additional allowances. In practice, the posts are distributed so that all senators and nearly half of the Assembly members receive extra compensation.

Every legislator is allotted office space. Leaders and a few major committee chairmen are accommodated in the Capitol Building; all others are across the street in the Legislative Office Building. In addition, members receive allowances for other offices in their home districts. The legislature also underwrites much of the cost of staff assistance, provides a bill drafting service and conducts a research office to help members.

The legislative budget appropriation for Fiscal Year 1988-89 was over $174 million. Legislative costs nearly tripled between 1979 and 1989.

SESSIONS OF THE LEGISLATURE

In contrast to some others, the New York State Legislature meets annually in unlimited session. It convenes at the Capitol in Albany on the first Wednesday after the first Monday in January and continues in session until a date mutually agreed upon by both houses. Neither house may recess for more than two days without the consent of the other. Generally legislators are in Albany three days a week, but, as the session advances, they are likely to meet more often. In recent years, sessions have lasted for six months or longer. As a relatively new phenomenon, the legislature has declined to adjourn formally when its work is completed. This permits its members to return at short notice to take up a special issue or overturn a veto. Some see the open-ended sessions as a step in the direction to a full-time legislature.

Special sessions, called extraordinary sessions, may be called by the governor. At such times, the legislature may act only on matters that the governor has put before it. However, in the absence of formal adjournment, the legislature can now return to regular session and its own agenda at any time, which considerably weakens the governor's control. Once a rare occurrence, special sessions have been used increasingly to address unfinished business.

Under a 1975 constitutional amendment, to date unused, the legislature may also be convened by its leaders if they have been so petitioned by two-thirds of the members. Only subjects enumerated in the petition may then be on the session agenda. The legislature is also automatically convened by notice from the Chief Judge of the Court of Appeals if charges for removal or retirement have been preferred against a judicial officer.

The legislature holds joint sessions—with both houses sitting together in the larger Assembly Chamber—to receive the governor's annual "State of the State" message and for the election of members of the Board of Regents. It also held a joint session to hear Chief Judge Sol Wachtler speak on the "State of the Courts."

The session is only the more visible part of legislative work. During the rest of the year, the lawmakers perform various services for their constituents, serve on committees and commissions which develop legislation, or even gather informally in "mini-sessions" to make plans for the coming session.

ORGANIZATION OF THE LEGISLATURE

The functioning of the legislature can be understood best in political terms. Legislators almost always belong to one of the two major political parties, although occasionally a legislator enrolled as Conservative, Liberal, or Right to Life receives a Democratic or Republican endorsement. Because majority and minority members sit on opposite sides of the Senate and Assembly chambers, a legislator will frequently refer to the opposition party as "the other side of the aisle."

Before the opening session, each party caucuses to select its nominees for officers of the Senate or Assembly. Dissension within a party, at times, has caused a contest over the leadership. Once that matter is decided, each party votes as a bloc on the organization of the legislature, a procedure which necessarily gives the majority party in each house the ability to name its officers and make the rules. Majority leaders then exercise effective control by making appointments, insuring that their members chair and dominate all committees with sufficient votes to pass or defeat measures. In effect, this means that minority members of each house can usually obtain passage of minor bills, but can only cosponsor significant legislation with the majority party.

At the opening session in January, after the oath of office has been administered, the newly elected members formally organize by voting on the decisions that have already been made in their presession caucuses. At that time, they also adopt rules that will govern their procedures for the two-year term. In either house, the rules may be amended at any time.

THE OFFICERS

The presiding officer of the Senate is the lieutenant-governor, who serves by virtue of his office. Under the constitution, he may not join the debate or vote on any question except to break a tie. Political control belongs to the majority leader.

Each party nominates a candidate to serve as Temporary President of the Senate, commonly referred to as the majority leader. The unsuccessful candidate becomes the minority leader. The majority leader has general supervision over the business of the Senate and appoints the chairman and members of all committees, as well as most of the administrative and auxiliary employees. The majority and minority leaders are generally the spokespersons for their parties and are responsible for shepherding their bills through the legislative process.

In the Assembly, the presiding officer is the speaker, elected by the members, upon the nomination of the majority party. The speaker is the center of power in the Assembly, directing the course of its business, ruling on parliamentary procedure, and certifying the passage of all bills. The speaker may leave the chair to debate on any measure, although it is rarely done, and may vote but is not required to do so except to break a tie. The speaker makes all committee assignments and appoints and directs the work of most of the Assembly staff.

The speaker's first official act is to appoint the majority leader of the Assembly who is floor manager for his party's legislative proposals. The minority leader performs duties similar to those of the minority leader of the Senate.

As soon as both houses are organized, each sends a select committee consisting of a member from each party to inform the governor that it is ready to proceed with business, and will meet in joint session to receive the annual message. The present custom is for the governor to deliver a message personally in the Assembly Chamber on the first day of the session. The governor reports on developments since the last session and recommends matters for attention during the new one. This annual message is a blueprint of the governor's legislative program that will be developed more fully in the budget message. After receiving the governor's message, the senators return to their own chamber, and the legislative session is officially underway.

THE COMMITTEES

Much of the work of the legislature takes place in its standing committees. The Senate Majority Leader and Assembly Speaker, in consultation with the minority leaders, appoint the members of these committees. Although seniority and the prestige of an individual legislator will influence his or her assignment, no fixed pattern or precedent governs the appointments. In all cases, the chair and a majority of committee members belong to the majority party.

Every bill begins (and sometimes ends) its progress through the legislature in one of these committees. No bill reaches the floor of either house for debate unless it has been "reported out" to the floor by a standing committee. But in many cases a committee will refer its important measures not to the floor but to the rules or finance committees (Assembly Ways and Means, and Senate Finance) of their respective houses, where leadership control resides.

The key committee in each house is the Rules Committee; the Senate Majority Leader and Assembly Speaker serve as the respective chairmen in both the Senate and Assembly. The membership of the rules committee is made up of the chair and ranking minority members of other important standing committees. These committees should not be confused with congressional committees of the same name which adopt a "rule" for each measure to determine when and how it may be debated.

The chief power of Rules in the state legislature is the forum it affords for leadership decision making. For the most part, bills that lack support of these few key legislators do not pass. Many of the formal procedures through which this power was once exercised have been changed and the autocratic image of the leaders modified, but the center of control is essentially unaltered. For example, Assembly standing committees are no longer required to report out all their bills on a date set by the speaker, but they continue voluntarily to transfer their most controversial business to Rules as adjournment approaches. In the Senate, the Rules Committee has authority to take over bills referred to any other committee but it rarely does so. Late in the session, after a compromise has been finally negotiated on a troublesome issue, only the rules committees have the ability to get the accepted version to the floor for action, for the rules committees alone may introduce bills after the deadlines for individual introductions have passed.

The ability to determine the order in which bills are presented for a vote, is another critical function of leadership, exercised as the session advances. Hundreds of measures just do not get into print until after the session has ended, in part because of the huge printing backlog, but in part because of their low priority to the leadership.

The finance committees, which have an input in any bill involving expenditure of state money, are the second significant repositories of leadership control. Important measures that are not referred to Rules are most often reported to the Finance Committee in the Senate, and to the Ways and Means Committee in the Assembly. The chairmen of committees that forward their bills in this manner are often members of either the finance or rules committees themselves.

In 1988, there were 32 standing committees in the Senate and 36 in the Assembly. Assembly committees generally have 18 to 22 members but range from seven to 38. Senate committees are usually smaller, ranging from seven to 23.

Most senators serve on six standing committees; members of the Assembly on three or four. Overlapping responsibility is thus built into the system. Few committees can expect full attendance at all meetings but they do meet regularly and give independent consideration to their assigned bills. Some say committee performance has been enhanced by the presence of the press and public. Unless two-thirds of the members vote for a closed session, all committee meetings are now open.

In spite of its large number of standing committees, the legislature appoints other groups to develop legislative proposals and policies. Among them are some permanent legislative commissions with both Senate and Assembly members. These have continuing responsibilities, such as the Commission on Expenditure Review and the Bill Drafting Commission.

Others are temporary joint legislative commissions, created by statute; or task forces created by resolution for a specific purpose and a limited term. Some may include nonlegislative members. All may hire staff, may give intensive attention to an issue outside the pressures and politics of the session, and may produce legislative recommendations. None, however, may introduce bills.

Each house also has its own select committees or task forces addressing issues that do not easily fit into a standing committee's jurisdiction. Examples are the Senate Select Committee on Casino Gambling and the Assembly Task Force on School Finance and the Real Property Tax.

CHAPTER 5
HOW A BILL BECOMES A LAW

When a legislative proposal is introduced in the Senate or Assembly, it is called a bill. At the legislative session of 1920, 3442 bills were introduced. Of these nearly twenty-seven percent, or 940 measures, were signed into law. Sixty-eight years later, in 1988, the number of measures presented to the legislature reached well over 21,000 but the number of bills signed into law amounted to about three percent of the total.

The vast increase in introductions over the past half-century reflects expanded activities of the state as well as a rise in the number of politically active pressure groups, each with its own legislative objectives. The decrease in the number of completed actions suggests that the legislature's capacity may be tied to factors other than the volume of introductions.

To become law, then as now, a bill must be passed in exactly the same form by both houses. It must then be sent to the governor for signing. Relatively few measures survive the pitfalls and complexities that surround each step in this process (see Figure 5-1).

WHO MAY INTRODUCE BILLS

Bills may be introduced in a number of ways:

- by a member or members of either house (most bills are introduced this way)
- on report of a standing committee or by the Rules Committee
- by order of either house (rare)
- by message from either house (When one house passes a bill, it is sent to the other house for action)
- by message from the governor (budget bills).

Not all legislation must originate with individual legislators, standing committees or the governor. A state department head, a lobbyist, or an individual citizen may actually draft legislation and ask a legislator to introduce it.

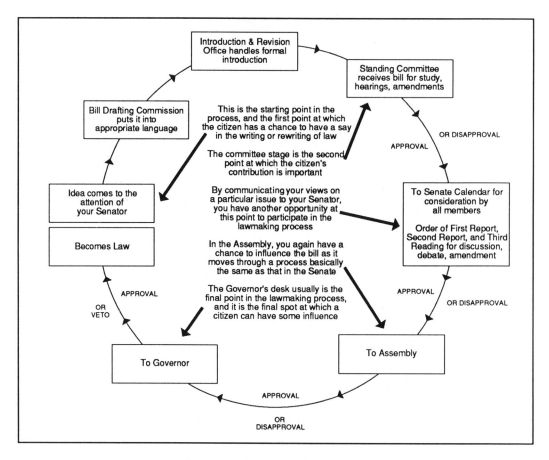

Figure 5-1: **How a Bill Becomes a Law**

A huge number of the introductions each year are "companion bills;" that is, identical bills each introduced with its own number, and its own sponsor, in each house who will presumably work actively for its passage. Other duplication occurs because each legislator wants to gain credit for sponsoring bills that are politically popular or are requested by a constituent or special interest group. This leads to the introduction of a large number of closely similar bills that may be put in year after year without much prospect for passage.

In an effort to cut down on the number of separate annual introductions and their accompanying printing costs, some bills that have not been acted on by the end of the first year of a two-year term of the legislature are now carried over and considered to be automatically introduced without reprinting in the second year. For the same reason, other methods of jointly sponsoring bills have been encouraged, including:

- multi-sponsored bills—those sponsored by two or more legislators in the same house
- uni-bills—printed only once and simultaneously introduced into both houses. The names of both their Senate and Assembly sponsors appear on the measure.

None of these devices has been of substantial help in reducing the volume of introductions. This volume is so great that few, if any, legislators can successfully follow all the bills during the legislative session. Recognizing a need for orderly supervision over this huge volume of legislative business, legislators continue to pass rules of the legislature which enhance the control the leaders exercise over the movement of legislation.

SCHEDULE FOR INTRODUCING BILLS

•Legislators may prefile bills between November 15 and the opening of the session. Prefiled bills are considered as introduced on the first day of the session but they are actually printed and ready for committee consideration when the legislature convenes. This practice, designed to speed up the session, in fact, has had little effect.

•In the Assembly, members may introduce as many bills as they please until the first Tuesday in March.

•Until the last Tuesday in March, each member of the assembly is limited to ten new introductions.

•The Senate follows a similar schedule. Senate deadlines, as fixed by the majority leader, usually follow Assembly deadlines by one week.

•Thereafter only the rules committees may introduce bills except where introductory numbers have been reserved for bills under preparation by individual legislators.

•A legislator, elected after the late March deadline, will have some opportunity to introduce bills.

THE PROGRESS OF A BILL

Bills may be introduced in either or both houses. When a bill is introduced, it is printed and is given a number which identifies it as it moves through the legislative process. The sponsor prepares a memorandum to accompany the bill, describing its purpose.

Each bill is assigned to an appropriate standing committee, which considers and reports on bills the chairperson has placed on the agenda. Thus, the committee chairman, often in consultation with the leadership, has great influence over matters that will ultimately reach the floor. However, new rules in the Assembly permit a sponsor to require a committee to vote on a bill.

If a bill is amended, a letter is added to its number (for example, Senate Bill S. 123 becomes Senate Bill S. 123-A after its first amendment). Each time a bill is amended, it is reprinted and a letter added. If a bill is amended in the opposite house it receives a special print number.

When a bill is introduced, it is said to be on first reading. If it is reported out of committee, it appears on the second reading calendar in the Assembly or on the General Orders calendar in the Senate. Each house prints a daily calendar of all bills reported out of committee. A bill cannot receive final action until it has been moved to the third reading calendar. A bill on third reading is ready to be acted on by the legislature.

No bill may be passed until it has been on the legislators' desks in printed form for three legislative days. However, if the governor sends a Message of Necessity to the legislature indicating that the bill should be considered at once, this aging process is waived. Even with a Message of Necessity, a bill must be on legislators' desks in final, though not necessarily printed, form before it can receive action. Toward the end of the session, it is not uncommon for legislators' desks to be covered with stacks of bills two feet high.

OBSTACLES TO THE PROGRESS OF BILLS

The leadership is the traffic manager for getting measures to the floor, but much may happen to a bill even after it appears on a third reading calendar, presumably ready for action. For example, third reading bills approved for action generally need to be marked in the daily calendar with an "H." This means they have been issued a "high print," or priority rating, by the leaders.

A bill may be stopped at the third reading stage if the introducer, or in the Senate, the majority leader, places a star next to its calendar listing. A starred bill cannot advance until 24 hours after the star is removed. Most sessions adjourn with hundreds of starred bills still on their calendars.

A bill may be amended any time until it has had its third reading. Actually, even after it has been passed, it can be amended by motion to reconsider the vote by which it passed. It can even be recalled from the governor's desk after it has passed both houses. Every session sees some of these recalls.

When a bill passes one house, it is sent to the other where it goes through an identical process. A bill may be amended in either house and returned to the other house for concurrence in the amendment. Sometimes, the Senate and Assembly pass measures that are similar but not identical. Although the rules provide for committees of conference to resolve differences between the two houses, this technique is not commonly used. In the absence of such a mechanism, it is possible for each house to pass its own version of a controversial or politically sensitive measure, then place the blame on the other house for failing to act.

PASSING THE BILLS

Most bills that get as far as a vote are noncontroversial and pass with very little dissent on either side of the aisle. Relatively few measures are ever presented for full floor debate. After the noncontroversial bills are disposed of, the house turns to the controversial measures. If there is to be debate, the time allotted each member is limited; none may speak more than twice on the same bill on the same day.

Positions on important bills may be reached at separate meetings, either conferences or caucuses of all legislators of each party. The leaders naturally exert great influence in these meetings. At one time, leaders could call on members to vote as a bloc on "party bills." Today such party allegiance is less easily commanded. Legislators are apt to be more attentive to their constituencies on controversial issues. However, legislators persistently voting in opposition to their parties can find themselves with poor committee assignments and lack of party support for their own measures.

COUNTING THE VOTE

A constitutional quorum must be present in the Senate or Assembly when a final vote on any bill is taken. In the case of most legislation, a quorum is a simple majority (one more than half) of all the elected members. If a bill imposes, continues, or revises a tax; creates a public debt; or appropriates public money, three-fifths of the members are needed for a quorum.

Most bills can be passed by a simple majority of the total membership of the house. A two-thirds majority is required to pass certain home rule bills, bills which appropriate public money or property for private or local purposes, and to override the governor's veto.

The constitution requires that the ayes and nays on every bill be recorded in a journal of proceedings. On noncontroversial measures, this record is accomplished through the "fast roll call" which means that the clerk reads the first and last name on the alphabetical list of members and the names of the majority and minority leaders. All present are presumed to have voted in favor of the bill. (In the Assembly, presence is recorded though an electronic attendance system.) Members may be recorded in opposition by raising their hands during fast roll call.

Fast roll calls often take place when the majority or minority leader indicates that there will be a party vote on a bill. In that case, members are recorded as voting according to party affiliation, unless they indicate a wish to be recorded with the opposition. Fifteen members in the Assembly and five in the Senate may force a "slow roll call" in which the vote of every member of the house is individually recorded. Votes on controversial measures are almost always taken by slow roll call.

In the final weeks or days of the session, a special calendar called the Rules Calendar appears. This is the action list. The bills on it represent the compromises that have been worked out in leadership councils. Most of these measures are accompanied by a Message of Necessity from the governor to hasten passage.

ACTION BY THE GOVERNOR

A bill may be sent to the governor when it has passed both houses. Upon receipt of the bill, the governor is given ten days to act on it. Bills sent within ten days of the end of the session must be acted on within 30 days after the last day of the session. Since final action is taken on most bills during the last two weeks, this 30-day bill-signing period is inevitably a very busy time.

In recent years, the legislature has recessed instead of adjourning when its major business is done. Technically, this does not give the governor the 30-day constitutional period that ordinarily would be needed to deal with the session's output. In practice, however, the legislature has delayed sending some of the bills, delivering them instead over a period of weeks to allow a reasonable time to consider the huge number of measures passed in the final days.

If the governor takes no action on a ten-day bill, it automatically becomes a law. If the governor disapproves or vetoes a ten-day bill, it can become law only if it is repassed by two-thirds vote in each house. If the governor fails to act on a 30-day bill, the bill is said to have received a "pocket veto." It is customary for the governor to act, however, on all bills submitted, and give reasons in writing for approving or disapproving important legislation.

In November 1988, the legislature declined to give the governor emergency powers to halt spending previously approved as a way of dealing with the state's alleged large budget deficit.

CONSTITUTIONAL AMENDMENTS

Proposed amendments to the New York State Constitution, or ratification of proposed amendments to the United States Constitution, are introduced as Concurrent Resolutions in both houses. They follow a path similar to that of ordinary legislation except that no action by the governor is necessary.

A proposed amendment to the New York State Constitution is acted on only after it has been referred to the attorney general for an opinion as to its effect on other provisions of the constitution. It must be passed by two separately elected (but consecutive) legislatures, with the second passage effected in the first regular session of a legislature's two-year term. It is then presented to the voters for approval at a general election. If it is approved, it takes effect in January, following the referendum.

CHAPTER 6
STATE FINANCES

The state's fiscal policies and practices are reflected in its annual budget which is basically a plan for collecting and spending public money. A comparison of budgets over a period of years will show rates of economic growth or decline as well as new approaches to state financing.

Budget comparisons will reveal shifts in the state's concept of its governmental responsibilities. Responding to public expectations for health and social welfare programs, New York's expenditures have risen dramatically since 1977-78. Together with rising labor costs, retirement systems for state employees, and inflation, such undertakings have seen the General Fund rise from $11.1 billion in 1977-78 to $25.1 billion in 1987-88 before transfers.

BUDGET MAKING

The state constitution provides for a strong executive budget. This requires the governor to prepare a comprehensive program for the state each fiscal year, showing both a plan of expenditures to implement proposals and an estimate of the revenue that will be available to support these expenditures. Through this budget-making procedure, the governor becomes the chief architect of the state's policies and programs. Annual consideration of the budget is the New York State Legislature's most important business. Moreover, the governor can exercise an item veto on any legislative appropriation throughout the session.

The governor is not entirely a free agent in developing fiscal plans, but is limited by restrictions in the state constitution on the way money may be spent. These include prohibitions against the gift or loan of state money or credit to private undertakings. However, the constitution lists many exceptions to this rule, allowing the state to support certain enterprises that provide aid to special classes of dependent citizens, or that promote a specified list of state responsibilities in such fields as education, health, welfare and retirement benefits. In addition, the governor must ask for specific voter authorization on every state bond issue, although other forms of borrowing, discussed below, do not require such a vote.

Within these strictures and under the governor's direction, the Division of the Budget in the executive department prepares the budget, a huge document that runs to 1000 or more pages and weighs nearly six pounds. In preparing it, each department submits its appropriation request to the Division of the Budget by early September for the coming fiscal period (April 1 to March 31). Beginning in late September, the Division of the Budget analyzes and evaluates these requests in detail, and later in the fall discusses them with representatives of the Senate Finance and Assembly Ways and Means committees.

Both the legislature and the Chief Judge of the Court of Appeals also submit estimates of their operating expenses to the governor who must insert these in the budget as presented. During this process, forecasts from the Department of Taxation and Finance and data from the Office of the State Comptroller assist the Division of the Budget in projecting the state's revenue for the coming fiscal year. By early January, a completed budget reflecting the governor's policies is ready for presentation.

The governor must submit a budget to the legislature by February 1 in each year following the election of a governor, and by the second Tuesday after the opening of the legislature in other years. With its submission, the governor delivers a budget message containing the broad outlines of program proposals and plans for new taxes or other sources of revenue. Specific legislation that will implement these proposals is introduced in the form of budget bills, although the measures describing how the programs work may be delayed until late in the session.

The legislature must act on the appropriation bills submitted by the governor before considering any others. It may strike out or reduce, but may not increase, the appropriations recommended in the governor's budget. It may add items provided each is "stated separately and distinctly" and refers to a single object or purpose.

The governor does not sign and cannot veto legislative action on budget items originated in the executive department. Appropriations for the legislature and judiciary, and separate items added to the budget by the legislature are subject to the governor's approval or veto.

The system results in a good deal of give and take between the governor and the legislature. The governor prepares the budget and recommends methods of financing it. If the legislature disapproves of the revenue raising methods advocated, the burden is on it to decide which program will be curtailed to reduce expenditures, or to propose alternative means of financing. If it wishes to add new items, it may create additional sources of revenue, but the governor must agree to these.

Both courses — curtailing of programs and adding new revenues — are frequently unpopular with the public. A political settlement must be reached between the governor and legislative leaders. In recent years, the influence of the legislature in the budget making process has grown due to the ability of its fiscal committees to develop independent evaluations and forecasts of revenues and expenditures. In fact, in the 1980s, some of the most significant decisions in the budget process, including the 1987 Tax Reform Act, originated in these fiscal committees. The legislature has also sought to improve its understanding of the programs it enacts by creating a Commission on Expenditure Review which reports each year on a specific area of state spending.

Despite the legislature's heightened fiscal sophistication, it is often difficult for its leaders to muster the votes necessary for a budget accommodation with the governor. Coalitions of suburban legislators may be protecting education aid while urban representatives or black caucuses may be bargaining on social welfare programs. Or individual legislators may be using their votes to bargain over a "conscience" issue such as abortion or capital punishment. Such interests sharply challenge the party discipline that leaders need to negotiate successfully with the governor.

The state's fiscal year ends on March 31, requiring a new budget to be adopted before April 1. This schedule forces major battles in midsession. In the past decade, various crises that have since become routine have caused the legislature to delay adoption of the budget for a week or so, but more often policy outlines are approved in April and the fine-tuning of political settlements occur in May and June before the close of the legislative session. These are usually reflected in a "joint" supplemental budget, which the governor works out with the legislature in the closing days of the session.

After a budget has been adopted, programs or agencies may encounter cost overruns. These must be covered by deficiency appropriations. A deficiency appropriation may add to a previously authorized appropriation which has expired or is expected to be inadequate. Early in each session, about two months before the fiscal year ends the legislature acts on a deficiency budget designed to carry the state's programs and departments through the remainder of the fiscal year.

Thus three budgets — the major planning budget, the supplemental budget and the deficiency budget — combine to make up the state's total budget.

Prior to 1981, the state's budgetary practices had been criticized from an accounting standpoint. However, the **Accounting, Financial Reporting and Budget Accountability Reform Act** of 1981 was enacted, which introduced a new dimension to New York State's financial accounting and reporting practices - the use of generally accepted accounting principles (GAAP). With the enactment of this reform, New York now presents its State Financial Plan and Executive Budget both on the traditional "cash" basis and in accordance with GAAP. State accounting and financial reporting are also required to be in accordance with these principles.

Also, as a result of the 1981 legislation, beginning in 1983 the state moved to an all-funds budget which greatly increased the scope of the state's financial plan. Debt service and programs financed through various kinds of borrowing are now budgeted annually through the Debt Service and Capital Projects Funds. Items like federal grants are now also required to be budgeted.

STATE INCOME AND EXPENDITURES

Unlike the federal constitution, the state constitution requires the governor to offer a balanced budget; that is, one in which revenues are sufficient to meet the proposed expenditures. New York State could never accumulate the huge kind of budget deficit that exists at the federal level. Most of the income for the state General Fund budget comes from current revenues derived from taxes, fees, and interest payments (see Figures 6-1 and 6-2). But the state receives at least 30 percent more than it raises in the form of general grants and aid. Much of the federal money is in matching funds which pass through state and local governments for health, education, and welfare programs.

STATE REVENUES (TEN YEAR GROWTH) General Fund ($ millions)				
	1977-78 actual	1987-88 actual	$ change	% change
PERSONAL INCOME	4476	13921	9445	211%
USER TAXES AND FEES	3710	6828	3118	84%
Sales and Use	2412	5281	2869	119%
Motor fuel	481	470	-11	-2%
Cigarette	335	401	66	20%
Motor vehicle fees	256	421	165	64%
Alcoholic beverage taxes and fees	185	178	-7	-4%
Highway use	41	77	36	88%
BUSINESS TAXES	1999	3431	1432	72%
Corp. franchise	1087	1562	475	44%
Corp. and utilities	450	894	444	99%
Insurance	198	426	228	115%
Banks	199	407	208	105%
Other	65	142	77	118%
OTHER REVENUES	290	1292	1002	346%
Real property gains	-	549	-	-
Estate and gift	163	460	297	182%
Real estate transfer	10	186	176	1760%
Parimutuel	116	96	-20	-17%
Other	1	1	0	0%
MISCELLANEOUS	420	1174	754	180%
TOTAL REVENUES	10895	26646	15751	145%

Figure 6-1

In 1987-88, for example, the state raised $26.6 billion of its own from taxes, fees and other sources, and received nearly $9 billion additional in federal money. The bulk of the federal payments are not appropriated in the General Fund portion of the budget but are part of the Special Revenue Fund portion.

Money from all these sources, which is channelled to the general fund is allocated in four principal ways (see Figure 6-3):

1. Grants to Local Governments. In fiscal year 1987-88 this accounted for 68 percent of the General Fund budget and goes to aid local governments and school districts. Much of it is designated for specific programs in fields of health, welfare, aid to the handicapped, and education, but a major portion is allocated through "formula" for school aid and for unrestricted aid to localities (See Chapter 7).
2. State Operations. In fiscal year 1987-88 this accounted for over 26 percent of General Fund expenditures. It pays for the staff and activities of state departments and agencies, and is often called "the operating budget."
3. General State Charges. These costs which accounted for almost 7 percent of General Fund budget are mandated either by statute, collective bargaining agreement or court order. The major portion of appropriations in this area funds fringe benefits for employees. A smaller segment funds fixed costs, including payments in lieu of taxes and judgments against the state.
4. Debt Service. Less than 1 percent of the General Fund budget reflects the costs to the state of short and long term borrowing and lease purchase contracts.

WHAT THE BUDGET PAYS FOR

The presentation of the entire state budget, known as "all-funds," provides a complete picture of state income and spending by category (see Figure 6-4). However, the distribution of General Fund spending provides the best indicator of state priorities since it primarily reflects the spending of tax dollars (see Figure 6-3). Of total General Fund spending more than 65 percent or $16.6 billion, is in the form of grants to local governments.

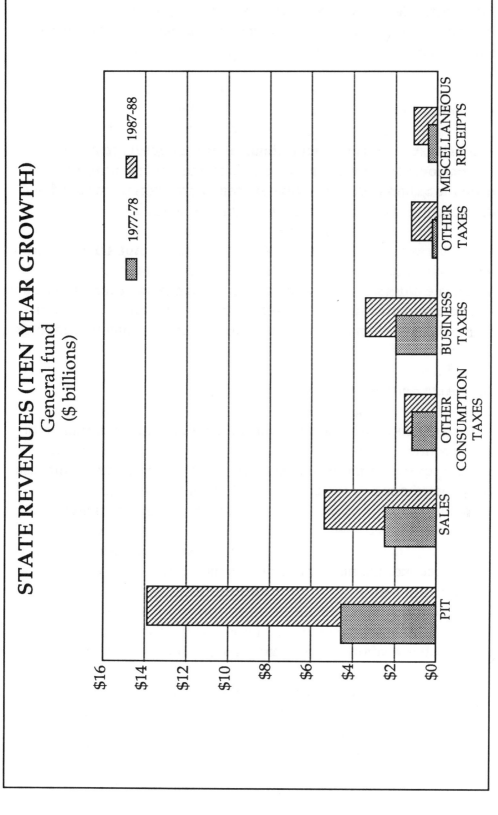

STATE REVENUES (TEN YEAR GROWTH)
General fund
($ billions)

1977-78   1987-88

$16
$14
$12
$10
$8
$6
$4
$2
$0

PIT   SALES   OTHER CONSUMPTION TAXES   BUSINESS TAXES   OTHER TAXES   MISCELLANEOUS RECEIPTS

Figure 6-2

Figure 6-5 provides a distribution of local assistance General Fund spending by function. Some of the major activities included in the categories named in Figure 6-5 are:

Education: State aid to local school districts; support for community colleges and the state university; state contributions to private institutions of higher learning and to the City University of New York (CUNY); educational television and some educational opportunity programs.

Environmental Conservation: Support for municipal waste treatment programs; managing land resources; setting standards for municipal and industrial discharges; monitoring and enforcing antipollution standards.

General Government: State support of the legislative and executive branches of government. (Localities share in the cost of the state judicial system.)

Health and Mental Health: Research and operational programs to combat pollution; aid for local health departments; support for facilities for treatment of tuberculosis, cancer, physical handicaps, sexually transmitted diseases; research into cancer detection, kidney ailments, and birth defects; monitoring occupational health hazards; facilities for treatment of mental health, addiction, and mental retardation.

Highways and Transportation: Construction and maintenance of highways; aid to localities for road maintenance, motor vehicles,and safety programs.

Housing and Community Development: Construction and maintenance of state-assisted housing, including New York City's Mitchell-Lama neighborhood rehabilitation and preservation programs; backing for Urban Development Corporation (UDC) investments on economic development projects; promotion of business and agricultural opportunity; and support for job-development loans to business.

Natural Resources and Recreation: Land acquisition programs for park and recreation; facilities for skiing, camping, swimming and other sports; historic site protection; parkway programs; protection of wildlife, fish, forest lands, and water resources; and protection of the forest preserve.

Public Safety: Crime control programs; maintaining correctional institutions; parole, probation and rehabilitation services; state police; national guard units and civil defense programs.

Service to Business, Labor and Agriculture: Programs of job development, assistance for small businesses; programs to attract new industry and promote tourism; and state agencies to provide for collective bargain-

NEW YORK STATE'S DOLLAR 1987-88
GENERAL FUND
(in Millions)

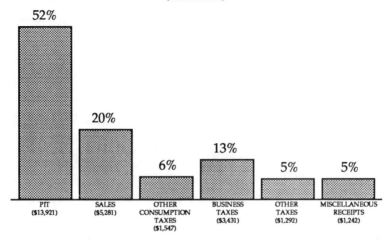

52%	20%	6%	13%	5%	5%
PIT ($13,921)	SALES ($5,281)	OTHER CONSUMPTION TAXES ($1,547)	BUSINESS TAXES ($3,431)	OTHER TAXES ($1,292)	MISCELLANEOUS RECEIPTS ($1,242)

WHERE IT COMES FROM

WHERE IT GOES

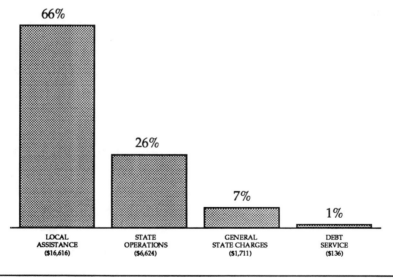

66%	26%	7%	1%
LOCAL ASSISTANCE ($16,616)	STATE OPERATIONS ($6,624)	GENERAL STATE CHARGES ($1,711)	DEBT SERVICE ($136)

Figure 6-3

ing services, manpower training and antidiscrimination programs, marketing information, consumer protection, control and prevention of plant and animal disease.

Social Services: Income assistance and health care for those who do not meet minimum standards of income; supplements federal aid for dependent children; programs for youth and the aging; and loan assistance for purchase of homes.

Within these categories, state payments are made through appropriations. Appropriations do not always coincide with expenditures, since less than the full amount may be spent within a particular fiscal year. The unspent part lapses and can no longer be used unless it is reappropriated by the legislature. If the unspent balance has been specifically committed, it may be used up to five and a half months after the close of the fiscal year. Because capital projects usually take more than one fiscal year to complete, reappropriations are often necessary.

BORROWING

Some of the money the state spends is obtained through borrowing. The state constitution requires that all full faith and credit state borrowing be submitted to the voters for approval and often such approval is hard to obtain. In view of this difficulty, a number of ways have evolved for contracting debt without referring it to the electorate.

Constitutional debt includes borrowing that has been subject to a referendum, as well as borrowing that is directly authorized by the constitution (such as that for public housing or job development). It also covers short term borrowing which the constitution authorizes for tax and revenue anticipation notes.

The most important short term borrowing occurs each spring before the state's income tax revenue begins to flow in. At that time, the state normally borrows two to three billion dollars to advance local assistance funds due to school districts and local governments. Recently, it has been suggested that New York State's fiscal year be changed to June 1. By that date, income tax revenues will be collected, eliminating the need for costly spring borrowing.

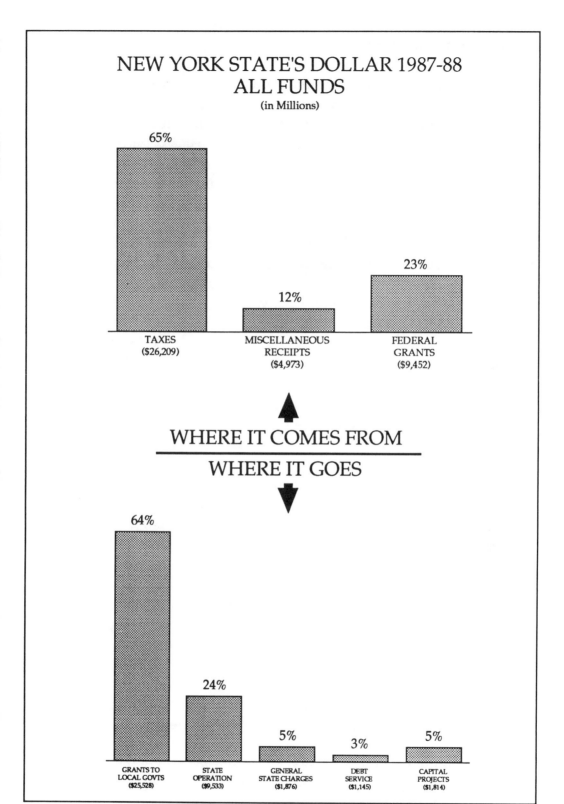

Figure 6-4

PUBLIC AUTHORITIES

In contrast, moral obligation debt has no such constitutional basis, though it is, in general,state supported. It finances a broad range of public benefit programs that are not to be found in the plan of state operations that we call the budget. Many are financed, constructed, and operated entities known as public authorities. These authorities perform essential government functions such as the building of housing and mental hygiene facilities.

Because authorities are legally private corporations, they are not subject to constitutional restrictions on the gift or loan of state money. For the same reason, state and local debt limitations do not apply to them and they may generally incur debt without voter approval. However, since the fiscal crisis of 1975, all public authorities (with the exception of the Municipal Assistance Corporation for the City of New York) have been limited as to the maximum amount of moral obligation debt that they may issue.

Public authorities, even those with local jurisdiction, are created by state law. Originally, their purpose was to construct revenue-producing facilities of a public benefit nature and to operate them on a self-sustaining basis. More recently, however, the legislature has also created authorities as a means of providing long-term financing for New York City and mortgage-guarantee-insurance financing to enable banking institutions to sell mortgages.

All of these authorities are subject to public regulation and their boards of directors are appointed by elected government officials such as the governor or a mayor. The statutes creating the moral obligation debt authorities often establish a procedure for the state to meet deficiencies that could arise in a corporation's debt service reserve fund.

In some cases the state does guarantee bonds issued by an authority, and here the voters must authorize the debt. State credit has been placed behind bonds issued by the Job Development Authority, the Metropolitan Transportation Authority and the Port Authority of New York and New Jersey, and such borrowing has been submitted to public referenda.

LOCAL ASSISTANCE ACCOUNT (1987-88)
(DISBURSEMENTS)
(in Thousands)

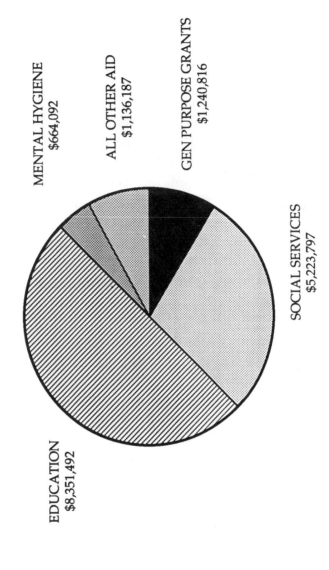

MENTAL HYGIENE
$664,092

ALL OTHER AID
$1,136,187

GEN PURPOSE GRANTS
$1,240,816

SOCIAL SERVICES
$5,223,797

EDUCATION
$8,351,492

Figure 6-5

By the 1970s there were about 32 major statewide public authorities with billions of dollars worth of assets and debt. This expansion was jolted in 1975 when the Urban Development Corporation, with more than $1 billion in debt outstanding defaulted on its notes, and the bond market was, at the same time, closed to New York City.

These events also closed the bond markets for a short time to the state's other major public authorities, and by implication of moral obligations debt, to the state itself. Soon thereafter the state undertook measures to oversee the financial stability of public benefit corporations, and bolster its own credit.

The steps included the organization of other funding sources, including state retirement funds, banks and insurance companies capable of redeeming outstanding short term authority debt. In addition, "capping" legislation was enacted to limit the amount of moral obligation debt that an authority may issue; and the Public Authorities Control Board (PACB) was created. This Control Board determines whether projects proposed for bond financing are consistent with state policies and projected needs, and whether they are financially secure. Nevertheless, the outstanding aggregate debt held at the end of fiscal 1986 by the 32 state wide authorities totalled $26 billion.

Clearly, authority financing must be taken into account in any evaluation of the state's fiscal operations or status. The public may pay more for facilities run by authorities because of the higher interest rates on their borrowing through bonds not guaranteed by the state. When state credit does stand behind authority bonds, there is a potential fiscal obligation which must be considered in the state's total debt picture even though this does not appear in the budget as a direct obligation. Some of the largest public authorities are the New York State Thruway Authority, the New York State Power Authority, the Port Authority of New York and New Jersey, the Housing Finance Agency, the Dormitory Authority, and the Metropolitan Transportation Authority.

LEASE PURCHASE

Another major form of borrowing is called lease-purchasing which has financed state office buildings, such as the Albany South Mall and other facilities in Binghamton and Utica. In these cases, municipal bonds were issued by the local government where the buildings are located. The municipality pays the debt service on the bonds with state money it receives for the state's lease-purchase of the facility. In 1979-80 the Executive Budget for the first time reported these rent-like obligations as part of the state's debt service picture, though the payments themselves are made through the Office of General Service. In 1988-89, such payments came to $77 million.

In addition, in 1985, equipment purchases for state departments and agencies began to be financed through notes known as Certificates of Participation (COPS). This method of financing is less expensive than straight lease purchase payments since it enables the state to access the more competitive interest rates of the short term money markets. As of December 1988, $360 million in COPS has been issued.

PART II

LOCAL GOVERNMENT

Local governments existed on the American continent before state and national governments were established and their structure and powers served as models for the larger bodies. Today under our federal system, the state is the political unit whose constitutional and statutory provisions determine the powers and the very existence of all local governments within its borders. Indeed, local governmental units are commonly called "creatures of the state," and the state supports and regulates their activities. Everyone who lives in the state is a resident of one of New York's 62 counties, a city or town, and a school district. With the exception of the five counties known as boroughs, which make up the City of New York, the territory of each county is wholly divided into cities and towns. Twenty-one counties have towns only.

A town may have one or more villages within its borders. Villages may lie in more than one town or even in more than one county, but a village may not lie within a city.

Counties, cities, towns, and villages are called general-purpose local governments because each provides a number of services. Because counties and towns were originally formed to serve as administrative arms of the state, they are known as involuntary subdivisions or units of government. Villages and cities, on the other hand, were formed at the request of their residents and are considered voluntary jurisdictions.

In addition to the 1600 general purpose local governments in the state, there are 734 school districts; 838 fire districts; many local and regional authorities; and hundreds of special districts, each of which provides a single service or a closely related group of services.

Local governments have been in existence in New York for over 300 years. In that time, they have evolved into a many-layered system that serves as the point of delivery for many national and state governmental programs. The sharing of responsibility with other levels of government emanates from the state constitution. State laws grant power and authority to local governments. For local governments to carry out such responsibility, however, requires adequate authority and fiscal resources. It is apparent in many cases that their ability to raise money has not kept pace with the growth of their responsibility.

In future years, local governments are likely to face ever greater challenges and stresses. Continuing revision of constitutional and state laws affecting local government will undoubtedly provide for future changes in local government organization, power, and capability to administer and finance public services.

CHAPTER 7
HOW MUNICIPALITIES OPERATE

HOME RULE

Home rule is the power granted to local governments by the state constitution to manage and control their own property, affairs, and government. Many local concerns, however, are also state concerns because of the state's constitutional responsibility to provide for the welfare of all its citizens and because of its role in financing services. Conflicts between the desire of local governments to handle what they consider to be their own affairs, and the state's attempts to set minimum and uniform standards become more intense every year. In the case of overlapping responsibilities, it is often difficult to determine which is the state and which the local function. Most often, when a matter is put to a court test, it is decided in favor of the state.

Since all units of local government are subdivisions of the state, their rights are only those granted by the constitution or by the legislature. The legislature may pass laws relating to local governments, subject to certain restrictions stated in the constitution. The "Home Rule" Article, for example, contains a "Bill of Rights for Local Governments." These include the right to have an elected legislative body; to adopt local laws; to elect or appoint local officers; to cooperate with other governments in providing services; to be protected against annexation of territory by other local governments; and to exercise the right of eminent domain.

These constitutional protections and grants of power are implemented in:

- **The Municipal Home Rule Law** which gives all counties, cities, towns and villages powers to adopt laws consistent with the New York State Constitution and general legislation. It spells out other local powers and simplifies the legislative amendment process.
- **A Statute of Local Governments** which prohibits the legislature from withdrawing or constricting powers it has granted to localities under the statute except by the passage of the same law in two successive years.

• **The Municipal Annexation Law** which guarantees that no local government, nor any part of its territory will be annexed by another unless a majority of the voters in the affected territory approve. The governing body of each local government involved also has to approve the annexation as being in the overall public interest. Cases of conflict between the local governing body and its voters may be taken to the Appellate Division of the Supreme Court.

Today, suburban towns and villages share problems with the cities. Municipal functions of all are affected not only by population density, but also by industrialization, transportation patterns, and environmental pollution. As different classes of local governments seek similar powers to deal with these problems, the distinctions between city, village, and town forms of government become much less sharp than they once were.

STATE-LOCAL FISCAL RELATIONSHIPS

In a broad sense, the state bears substantial responsibility for its subdivisions. They are required by the constitution to place their full faith and credit behind all debt; they may not give or loan money or extend credit to any private enterprise or individual. State laws spell out in close detail the conditions under which local governments may borrow, tax, and account for their expenditures.

But the state's role in municipal financing was dramatically underscored in 1975 as New York City's tangled financial affairs threatened its solvency. When the city was unable to raise money for its capital needs, or sell its notes and bonds to investors, the governor proposed and the legislature created the Municipal Assistance Corporation (MAC) to sell bonds for the city that would be backed by the state's credit.

Because this action linked the state's financial welfare to the city's, the legislature also created the Financial Control Board (FCB) to exercise controls and supervision over the city's fiscal planning. New York City continues to decide on its own programs and expenditures but the FCB must determine whether these expenditures are consistent with the financial plan.

The Financial Control Board consists of the governor, the mayor, the state and city comptrollers, and three citizens appointed by the governor with the advice and consent of the Senate. The state has also intervened for a shorter period to support and supervise the City of Yonkers.

LOCAL GOVERNMENT EXPENDITURES

Expenditures by state and local governments in New York State conform generally to national trends. The costs of local government in New York State doubled between 1970 and 1980. In 1984, they were up nearly 26 percent compared to 1980.

Rising personal incomes and expectations have had the effect of broadening the scope of public services in education, environmental control, and highways. Expenditures for social services and health, under programs mandated and partly financed by state and federal governments, have greatly increased. Population changes have meant new programs for local governments throughout the state.

Central cities focus on transportation access, renewal or rehabilitation, housing, upgrading municipal services, and deteriorating infrastructure (see Chapter 11) and facilities. They are looking for ways to conserve their existing residential, commercial, and industrial assets and to attract and hold new enterprises.

Urbanized areas, more generally, are concerned with community development, the extension of necessary municipal services, the installation of public improvements, assimilation of economic activity, and other typical demands of growth.

The growing fiscal problems of central cities and other municipalities have resulted in a shift of some functions to county level government in many areas of the state. State and federal mandates have particularly affected county costs.

PROPERTY TAX

The property tax in New York State is based on the value of real property (land and improvements). It is the largest single revenue producer in the state tax system, yielding $11.65 billion in 1984 for local governments. It occupies a special place in the financing of local government not only because of its yield in relation to total local revenue, but also because of its key position in the municipal budget process.

Local government budgeting follows a procedure which first estimates expenditures or appropriations and then deducts estimated revenues from sources other than the property tax to arrive at a remainder, which is the tax levy. Thus the property tax levy is the balancing item on the revenue side of the municipal budget. The final step is fixing the local tax rate. The tax levy is divided by the total dollar amount of the assessed valuation of real estate within the local government. The result is a percentage figure, which is expressed as a tax rate, normally so many dollars and cents per $1000 of assessed valuation.

Where the tax levy for a county or school district is spread among a group of municipalities, assessed valuations are equalized for each municipality through the use of equalization rates. Equalization insures equity where property tax is levied over several local government units that assess properties at different percentages of full value or fair market value. The equalization rate in most cases is determined by the New York State Board of Equalization and Assessment.

As a municipality's fixed costs rise for social security, unemployment insurance and pension benefits, a number of them have bumped against their constitutional tax ceilings. Under pressure from their home communities, state legislators have tried various ways to overcome these tax limits but none has met success.

STATE AND FEDERAL AID

The local finance dilemma has fed a major debate over the responsibility of local governments for state mandated policies and programs, and of state government for such federal programs as welfare assistance. Squeezed between rising costs and insufficient power to raise revenue, municipalities tend to appeal to federal and state government, with their broader tax bases, for increased aid.

The state and federal governments generally designate the purpose and manner in which their aid money may be spent. For example, federal grants-in-aid for special programs require the local governments that receive them to meet specified requirements. Such special purpose federal aid is often integrated and coordinated with state aid.

Similarly, when state aid is delivered for specified purposes it is referred to as categorical grants-in-aid. Started years ago, categorical aid was established because of a concern for the general welfare and state interest in certain local government programs. The intent of categorical aid is to encourage local governments to establish programs to better serve their populations and to provide some uniformity in services across the state. A grant of this sort usually requires local matching funds.

Fifty-five percent of all state aid in fiscal year 1985 was for education. Categorical aid for social services accounted for 15 percent of total state aid, while 18 percent went to a variety of 63 other categorical aid programs.

The major program of general purpose aid from the state is known as per capita revenue sharing aid. This aid can be defined as financial aid to the support of local government functions without limitation as to its use. General purpose aid in fiscal year 1985 comprised 11 1/2 percent of total state aid.

In addition to its special and supervised aid, the federal government between 1972 and 1986 extended revenue sharing, or "no strings" aid. Through its array of categorical grant programs and revenue sharing, the federal government in the sixties and seventies transferred substantial sums to state and local governments. Federal aid, however, began to decline in 1980.

Through their power to set standards and provide funds, federal and state governments continue to have a growing impact on the nature and extent of local services.

PERMISSIVE TAXES

Local government expenditures climbed at a rate faster than the state's during the 1970s. To relieve home owners of part of the burden of supporting these costs, the legislature enacted permissive legislation to provide some property tax relief for those with small, fixed incomes. Municipalities and school districts may now grant 50 percent property tax exemption to elderly home owners whose income falls within stated limits. Various kinds of state aid are designed to offset, in part, the revenue loss that these exemptions cause to local governments.

New York State municipalities may also impose a variety of nonproperty taxes, including a sales tax; a one percent levy on the gross income of public utilities; taxes on coin-operated machines and hotel rooms; and in New York City, a modified income tax, as well as certain financial and commercial rent taxes.

SPECIAL CHARGES, FEES, AND EARNINGS

Local governments in New York State derive substantial revenues from special charges, fees, and earnings of municipal enterprises. Fees and charges often include interest and penalties on taxes, licenses, permits, departmental fees and charges, fines and other items. Earnings of municipal enterprises and special activities include revenues of such operations as water service, bus transportation, airports, hospitals, stadiums and public auditoriums, off-street parking, and municipally owned public utilities.

Local governments have wide latitude in establishing user charges. Municipalities have found it profitable to reexamine their charges periodically and bring them in line with current costs.

Off-track betting (OTB), set up by the legislature in 1970, provides revenues to counties and larger cities which participate in off-track parimutuel betting on horse races.

EQUALIZATION AND ASSESSMENT

Assessment

The taxing and borrowing powers of local governments and school districts, as well as the payment of various state aid, are based on the value of their real property. Each city and town and some villages (other than in Nassau and Tompkins Counties, where assessment is done at the county level) establish the assessed value of their own property. Until 1981, the **Real Property Tax Law** required all assessment to be at full value. Historically, however, real property in this state was usually assessed at a percentage of full value. Inequities have long existed among and within different classes of property, for example, residential, industrial, or commercial.

In the 1970s, these inequities stimulated a series of court challenges to the property tax assessment system of the state. Prompted by severe judicial criticism of assessment administration, the New York State Board of Equalization and Assessment prepared detailed analyses of assessment reform. Legislation was passed to set a time frame for assessing real property at full value. State financial assistance for reassessment was approved and a temporary state commission set up to study the impact of implementing the full value assessment standard. The time frame for implementation of full value assessment was extended several times by the legislature.

The temporary state commission, in its report of 1979, recommended assessment of property at full value. Recognizing that this would likely shift a substantial burden of the real property tax to residential property owners, the commission recommended consideration of a series of tax policy alternatives, such as circuit breakers and homestead exemptions, to soften the potential shift in burden.

Contrary to these recommendations, the legislature in 1981 repealed the full value assessment requirement of the Real Property Tax Law. This legislation authorized retaining fractional assessment using a uniform percentage of value for the assessment of each parcel of property. In addition, except in New York City and Nassau County where a classification system is prescribed, cities, towns, and villages are authorized to reduce the tax burden on residential dwellings for three or fewer families relative to other types of property. Thirteen municipalities had enacted two-tier tax systems by early 1986 which provided for a reduced tax burden on residential dwellings compared to business and industrial properties.

Because fractional assessment differs from place to place and within a community, the state establishes and applies an equalization rate designed to make assessments among different local governments comparable in terms of full value.

Equalization

The equalization rate is the percentage of full value at which the State Board of Equalization and Assessment judges the locality to be assessing its property. In this process, local assessment rolls are checked, data studied, and local assessors consulted to determine the levels of assessment and changes made since the previous year.

A local government's equalization rate also determines the amount it can tax and borrow. For example, a village's debt limit is based on 7 percent of its average full valuation (assessed value divided by the state equalization rate) over a five year period. Therefore a lower equalization rate results in an increased full value computation and, consequently, a higher debt limit.

There continues to be a need to raise the quality of local property tax systems and administration. Efforts at both the local and state level have resulted in many municipalities taking corrective action to remove assessment inequities. Better assessor training has been provided, records have been improved, and new tax maps have been made. In many assessment jurisdictions across the state, however, wide differences still exist among classes of property and within classes of property.

STATE-LOCAL ADMINISTRATIVE RELATIONSHIPS

Frequently, the administration of state laws is in the hands of local officials. A most familiar example is the district attorney and sheriff in each county who carry out state law and are considered to be state officers for some purposes. While they are the chief law enforcement officers of the county, locally elected and locally responsible, they may be removed by the governor for misconduct or neglect of duty.

All New York State counties (except Nassau and Westchester) elect sheriffs who have responsibility for county law enforcement activities. The sheriff works closely with state police officers, who sometimes assume the responsibility for apprehending criminals and enforcing regulations within the county.

Many local commissioners, for example, Social Service, are appointed locally but administer both county and state services and disburse both county and state funds. Rules governing elections are set by the state and carried out by county boards of elections and by the New York City Board of Elections.

The administration of civil service is partly a state and partly a local duty. Cities and counties administer the Weights and Measures Law. Dog licenses and hunting licenses are regulated by the state but issued by city, town, and village clerks.

When problems arise in the administration or funding of state-local programs, an individual mayor, supervisor or executive may appeal to the appropriate legislators or state agencies for relief. The legislative objectives of all municipalities are vigorously pursued in Albany each year by such state-wide organizations as the Conference of Mayors, Association of Towns, Association of Counties, and School Board Associations.

THE COUNTIES

The role of county government has undergone continuous evolution since colonial times. In New York State counties were first established as a basis for representation to the Colonial Assembly and as judicial districts. When the need arose for public buildings, such as courthouses and jails, the supervisors of the various towns in the county were assembled so that the cost could be apportioned. This was the origin of the county board of supervisors which still serves as the legislative body in some counties.

After the Revolutionary War, as settlers fanned out through the state, new counties were created, generally as soon as the population reached 1000. The last, Bronx County, was created by the legislature in 1914. No new county may be formed by the legislature unless it has a population at least equal to that of an Assembly district. But counties have grown in power if not in number as their populations have increased and as their governments have become more complex.

Today, county government performs vital services, both as a local government and as an administrative arm of the state. Growth and change of function have taken place at an uneven pace, however, and county government structures vary widely across the state. A most important mechanism in the developing role of counties has been their ability, since 1963, to adopt charters; create and abolish county departments and agencies; make appropriations and levy property, sales, and other taxes; and provide generally for many governmental functions.

In the past 40 years, counties with extensive urban development have taken on a vast array of new services. Some services which were originally carried out by cities, towns, and villages within the county were consolidated at the county level; others were the result of new or increasing problems, such as solid waste management, caused by population growth and environmental concern. In some cases, cities urged counties to assume activities, such as parks, zoos, and civic centers, not only to spread the cost more equitably since all county residents are likely to use such facilities, but also because the county has greater ability to finance such activities.

Through the adoption of a charter, the county may augment its powers considerably. A charter may divide legislative and executive responsibility, and provide for agencies and officers to perform various county operations. Nineteen counties in New York have adopted charters. Of these, 18 have established an executive officer, all but two of whom are elected. Even among noncharter counties, some legislative bodies are hiring professional administrators to deal with the increasingly complex functions of county government. Noncharter counties operate under the authority of **New York State County Law**.

The struggle for county home rules has a long history in New York State. In the late 1930s, the home rule movement among local governments resulted in charters for Nassau and Westchester counties by special constitutional authorization and legislative grant. Monroe County adopted a charter under a general law providing for alterative forms of government.

Under the Home Rule Article of the New York State Constitution, as revised in 1938 and later in 1963, counties outside the City of New York may now draft and adopt their own charters by action of their legislative bodies subject to the approval of the voters. To become effective, however, a county charter must be approved by the voters of the cities considered as one unit and also by the voters outside the cities considered as one unit.

If the proposed charter would also transfer a function to or from a village in the county, the change would also have to be approved by a majority of voters in all of the villages affected. Thus, a county charter proposal may be subject to triple referendum, and county reorganization may be vetoed by voters in any one of three classes of local government, even though those voters may not constitute a majority of the total number voting on the question.

The legislative body of a county was traditionally a board of supervisors consisting of the supervisor of each of the towns and of supervisors elected, usually by wards, from the cities who had no function other than to represent that city in the county legislature. Application of the one man, one vote principle to county legislative bodies revolutionized the concept of county government. In most cases, representation to a county legislative body is now from single or multimember districts based on population. In other cases, a supervisor may cast a vote weighted to reflect the population in the town.

Legislative bodies of counties are variously known now as boards of supervisors, boards of representatives, boards of legislators, county legislatures, and legislative boards.

Other elected officials in counties include a district attorney, a sheriff, a county clerk, coroner(s), and a treasurer. The position of coroner may be replaced with an appointive medical examiner and the office of treasurer may be dropped and its functions performed by the position of director of finance. The office of sheriff may be substantially modified.

Like some other local governments, counties are subject to constitutional restrictions on their tax and debt limits. On the other hand, they attract substantial state and federal aid because of the regional services they provide. As local governments that can function on area-wide bases, it appears that counties will continue to assume new responsibilities for the rest of the century as they respond to the increasing pressures of an urban society.

THE CITIES

New York State has 62 cities ranging in size from under 3000 to over 7,000,000 persons. Their geographic areas range from 0.9 to 303.7 square miles.

Cities are municipal corporations established and defined by their charters. Albany and New York City, the state's earliest cities, received royal charters in 1686. Since then, city charters may be granted only by the legislature. Once it has adopted a charter, a city may revise or obtain another by following procedures set forth in the Municipal Home Rule Law. There are at present 62 cities in New York State (see Figure 7-1).

Many cities developed along the principal trade route of the state, the Hudson-Mohawk arterial between New York City and Buffalo and most are on sites which were once trading or junction posts. Historically, cities came into being to provide the services necessary for areas of concentrated population, but it is difficult to generalize about their structures. To begin with, there are broad differences in the charters granted to them by the legislature. Even cities with similar forms of government differ widely in practice. Their population range reinforces the differences. Although popular thinking tends to regard cities as larger and more densely populated units, this is not necessarily true in New York State where many towns and villages are larger than some cities.

In general, city government falls into four broad categories:

1 *Strong mayor-council,* under which an elective mayor is the chief executive and administrative head of the city and the council is the policy-making body. The mayor usually has the power to appoint and remove agency heads, with or without council con-

firmation; to prepare the budget; and to exercise broad veto powers over council actions. This form sometimes includes a professional administrator appointed by the mayor and is then called the "mayor-administrator plan."

2 *Weak mayor-council*, under which the mayor is mainly a ceremonial figure. The council is not only the policy-making body, it also provides a committee form of administrative leadership. It appoints and removes agency heads and prepares budgets. There is generally no mayoral veto power.

3 *Council-manager*, under which an appointed, professional manager is the administrative head of the city, the council is the policy-making body and the mayor is mainly a ceremonial figure. The manager usually has the power to appoint and remove department heads and to prepare a budget, but does not have veto power over council actions.

4 *Commission*, under which commissioners are elected by the voters to administer the individual departments of city government and together form the policy making board. In some cases, one of the commissioners assumes the ceremonial duties of a mayor on a rotating basis.

In 1981, 41 cities in New York State had mayor-council governments, 18 had council-mayor governments, and three operated by commissions.

All cities have elected councils chosen at the November election in odd-numbered years. Elections are by wards, at-large, or a combination of the two. Mayors elected by the voters are elected at-large. City voters also elect city court judges outside of New York City. All cities have elected school boards except New York, Yonkers, and Rensselaer.

The five largest cities (New York, Buffalo, Rochester, Yonkers and Syracuse) vary from the remaining 57 because their school districts do not have the power to tax, but depend on city tax collection. They differ, too, in their constitutional tax and debt limitations. The problems of large cities in the state reflect many complex elements of social change, but population changes are often seen as both the cause and effect of these problems.

All of the states' large cities experienced rapid growth between 1900 and 1930. The surge in population was accompanied by a corresponding development in the city facilities and services. All cities built schools, roads, libraries, sewers, water systems, parks, and many other facilities.

This rapid growth tapered off during the depression decade between 1930 and 1940, and in the 30 years from 1940 to 1970 declined by 50 percent. Most cities experienced a population decline between 1970 and 1980. This stabilization and subsequent decrease of population in the central cities has been accompanied by residential growth in the surrounding suburban communities. Commerce and industry became decentralized as businesses and industry located outside the cities.

A transformation in the characteristics of the urban population has made cities the home of a larger proportion of ethnic minorities than other areas, of more persons of lower incomes and of persons in the youngest and oldest age groups (under 5 and over 65), all of whom present city governments with new challenges. Due to the greater age of New York's cities, the problems of physical blight, substandard housing, unemployment, crime, and environmental pollution are often more severe than elsewhere.

The cities generate much of the state's revenues, but also provide the most costly services, have the highest labor costs, the largest ratio of those needing public assistance, and the greatest number of tax exempt properties. It has become difficult for cities to provide all the services expected of them, as their ability to raise money has not kept pace with their need to provide new and expanding services.

NEW YORK CITY

Because of its size, both in area and population, New York City's government differs from the other cities of the state. Within the city borders are five counties, also known as boroughs, and about 7.3 million people. It has one mayor and a central legislative body. Each borough is represented in the city government by a borough president.

The politics of the city are unique because each party has five county organizations, but no citywide leader. This means that there are often primary contests for citywide office. If no primary candidate receives 40 percent of the party's vote there is a runoff primary between the two receiving the most votes. The mayor is usually regarded as the leader of his party.

The 1975 **New York City Charter**, amended by the voters in 1988, was expected to be fully implemented in 1989. Further revisions are anticipated after the Supreme Court renders its decision in 1989 on the application of the one person, one vote principle to the Board of Estimate.

The charter continues a strong mayor-council form of government and is intended to strengthen citizen participation in the city's affairs. The mayor has authority to appoint one or more deputy mayors and the heads of most departments, who serve at his pleasure. Appointments to certain boards and commissions are made with the advice and consent of the city council which must act within 30 days.

The mayor is responsible for preparing the expense budget and a separate capital budget, prepared by the New York City Planning Commission to cover capital construction costs.

The city council, the legislative arm of the government, consists of the council president and 35 council members elected from each of the 35 council districts. Under the charter, the city council has all the usual powers to adopt local laws. It may override the mayor's veto by a two-thirds vote.

New York City has a second deliberative body with predominantly fiscal responsibilities. This is the Board of Estimate, composed of eight city officials: the mayor, the comptroller and the president of the city council with two votes each; the five borough presidents, elected on a borough basis, have one vote each.

In addition to acting on the city's expense and capital budgets, the Board of Estimate controls zoning and planning; contracts, franchises; use and disposal of city property; rates for water, wharfage, lease of city property, and the city's employee retirement system. It may reduce assessments, taxes, and water rents levied on properties owned by charitable and educational organizations and it may approve sites for public and private housing projects.

The city council acts on both the capital and expense budgets with the Board of Estimate by holding joint public hearings on each proposed budget. The mayor may not take part in any action or vote on the budgets. A legislative Office of Budget Review analyzes department requests, budget changes, tax proposals, and capital borrowing for the council and the Board of Estimate. The mayor is given an item veto over all changes (including the refusal to appropriate sums for a specific purpose as well as reductions in amounts requested). The veto may be overridden only by a two-thirds vote of either body and a majority of the other. If the mayor's veto is not overridden, the item is deemed approved as originally proposed by the mayor.

The city's capital budget describes what the city will buy or build: subway cars, fire engines, roads, school buildings, or city institutions. It depends on bond revenues.

The city's expense budget covers the cost of day-to-day operations — salaries, maintenance, supplies, and interest on borrowing. It is a program budget and its line-item schedules are designed to let the mayor and the city's legislators know how an agency will proceed with its programs.

The City Planning Commission is responsible for preparing a draft capital budget for the mayor to submit to the Board of Estimate and city council. It is also charged with adopting a master plan for the physical development of the city; it is responsible for the city map and for zoning regulations, though it may be overridden on the latter by a three-fourths vote of the Board of Estimate. All of the city's fiscal planning is subject to review by the state-created Financial Control Board (FCB).

The Financial Control Board consists of the governor, the mayor, the state and city comptrollers, and the three citizens appointed by the governor with approval of the state Senate. The FCB has extensive power over the city. While it may not dictate how the city can spend its money or what services it can provide, it does determine whether the city is staying within approved budget allocations and can disapprove certain items which would imbalance the budget or jeopardize the city's long-range fiscal plans.

The city is divided into 59 community districts, each with its own unsalaried community board. Up to 50 members are appointed to each board by the borough president, half of them on the nomination of council members. These boards hold public hearings and make recommendations on land use in the district and on district budget priorities. They appoint a salaried district manager who presides over a cabinet composed of representatives of agencies that provide local services, city council members in the district, a representative of the city planning department and the chairperson of the community board.

A **School Decentralization Law**, enacted by the New York State Legislature in 1969, established a seven-member Central Board of Education. One member is appointed by each borough president, and two by the mayor. Members serve four-year terms.

The city is now divided into 32 community school districts, each of which elects nine members to a district school board under a system of proportional voting. Voters in this system do not have to meet usual voting qualifications, including that of citizenship, but need only be residents or parents registered to vote in the community school district. The central board and the community boards share administrative and policy-making powers in elementary, intermediate and junior high schools. The central board has sole power over the high schools and special school services.

There is also a Board of Higher Education, made up of seven members appointed by the mayor and seven appointed by the governor who act together to choose a chairperson.

THE TOWNS

A town is a subdivision of the county; the number of towns in a county ranges from three in Nassau County to 32 in Cattaraugus County. There are 932 towns in the state, varying in population from three-quarters of a million to 32 people. Towns are divided into three classes: suburban, first, and second. At one time there were major differences in powers among the various classes of towns but at present, differences in structure and powers have virtually disappeared. Towns operate under **New York State Town Law.**

In addition to the traditional role of towns of administering elections, maintaining highways, and administering judicial functions, towns through home rule powers and local laws may restructure their administrative organization to provide a wide variety of services.

While about half the towns in the state remain largely rural with populations under 2500, those towns that have experienced suburban population growth have often been pressured by new residents, used to services in cities, to provide water, sewage disposal, refuse collection, street lighting, recreation facilities, and many other services. Town government structure has shown a remarkable ability to provide these new and expanded services, sometimes on a townwide basis, sometimes on a town-outside-village (TOV) basis, and sometimes through special districts.

Older towns often face problems similar to cities. The ability of towns to raise revenues to meet their needs has been strained by an aging infrastructure and population shifts, either to revitalized city areas or to more rural areas.

The legislative body of a town is the town board which is usually composed of a supervisor and four council members. Council members, or town board members, are usually elected at large; although towns may provide by local law, subject to referendum, for representation from districts. A distinguishing feature of town government organization is the absence of a strong executive branch. The town board exercises both legislative and executive functions, with the supervisor exercising mainly administrative duties.

A town may, however, restructure its form of government to form a separate executive or administrative branch. Offices such as town executive or town manager may be established.

Town citizens elect two town justices to serve in their town courts. Nassau and Suffolk Counties, however, have district courts rather than town courts.

The offices of town clerk, highway superintendent, and receiver or collector of taxes are also elected unless a town, through local law and referendum, has made them appointive. Assessors are also either elected or appointed.

In preparing and adopting a budget, a town board, like other local governments, is limited by constitutional restrictions on borrowing. However, there is no limitation on powers of towns to tax real property.

Towns with villages often provide services, similar to those provided by the villages, to the areas outside the villages and charge the costs only to the areas receiving the services. Common town-outside-village activities include the regulation of subdivisions and review of development site plans, adoption of zoning ordinances and the administration and enforcement of them, and the construction and maintenance of streets and highways. Some highway costs, however, are charged townwide even though the village residents may not benefit directly.

Except for a small number of districts established prior to 1932 which have elected district commissioners, town boards administer all town special districts. (These do not include school and fire districts which are separate local government entities.) (See Chapter 8.)

THE VILLAGES

The state has more than 557 incorporated villages ranging in size from a population of 16 to more than 40,000 inhabitants. Twelve villages function under special charters; all others function under the **New York State Village Law**. This law, recodified in 1973 so as to be compatible with the Municipal Home Rule Law, provides for a broad and uniform grant of powers to village boards of trustees.

Historically, villages were created because clusters of people in otherwise sparsely settled towns wanted to secure fire or police protection or other public services. In the first 40 years of the twentieth century, as people moved from cities into suburbs, more than 160 villages were incorporated. Since 1940, however, only 19 new villages have been formed while several have dissolved. This change has come about largely through the use by towns of special improvement districts, which provide services to a section of a town and charge the costs of the service to the property owners in that section. (See Chapter 8.)

The legislative body of a village is the board of trustees composed of a mayor and four trustees, unless this number is changed by local law and referendum. The board has broad powers to raise money and to provide services. The mayor serves as executive of the village except in 46 villages where the position of manager or administrator has been created.

Other village officers include a clerk and a treasurer, appointed by the mayor with the approval of the board of trustees, unless local law provides otherwise. Some villages have provided for the elective office of village justice; those who have not, use the courts of the town(s) in which they are located.

Larger villages have multi-departmental organizations similar to cities to handle a broad range of services, while small villages may employ only a few individuals to handle basic road repair and snow removal. Some villages operate their own public utility plants. There are a number of town-village cooperative arrangements for a provision of some services.

TOWN-VILLAGES

A relatively new phenomenon in local government structure is the town-village, once limited to two jurisdictions in the state. Now a few others are weighing the merits of consolidation, chiefly to take advantage of the economy of unified services and fewer employees. Another impetus to change is the dissatisfaction expressed by many village residents at paying town taxes for services that chiefly benefit those outside the village boundaries. Governmental consolidation of this kind is subject to referendum, and in some cases, action by the New York State Legislature.

REGIONAL GOVERNMENTS

The multiplicity and complexity of local governmental patterns have increased in direct proportion to the urbanization of the state. Interlocking layers of county, city, town, and village governments, sewer, fire and other special districts have been created to supply services to expanding metropolitan areas. Effective planning and development on an area basis are difficult, and pressures are building for new ways to solve the common problems of communities.

The Tri-State Planning Commission is an interstate agency created to address problems of land use, housing, and transportation in the New York City metropolitan area. It has been designated as the agency to approve federal funding for any such projects that may affect regional planning. It seeks cooperation of public and private agencies involved in transportation and other regional facilities. While it does not itself operate any such facilities, it conducts surveys, develops proposals, and undertakes demonstration projects.

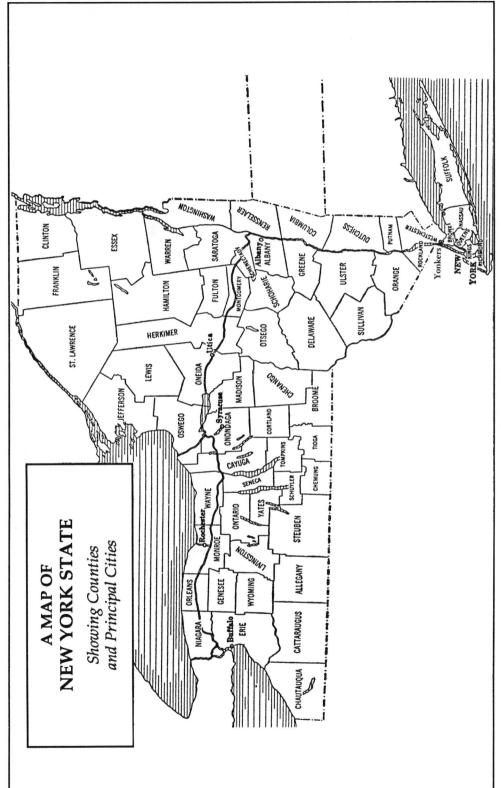

A MAP OF
NEW YORK STATE

*Showing Counties
and Principal Cities*

Figure 7-1

CHAPTER 8
LOCAL DISTRICTS AND AUTHORITIES

No examination of how local government operates would be complete without a description of districts and authorities. Local districts and authorities have one thing in common - each district and each authority exists to provide a single service. Districts fall into three categories: school districts, fire districts, and special improvement districts.

SCHOOL DISTRICTS

Just as the entire area of the state is divided into counties, and the counties into towns and cities, so the entire area of the state is divided into school districts. The boundaries of these districts do not necessarily coincide with town, city, village, or even county boundaries, except in the case of the larger cities. School districts are described in Chapter 9.

FIRE DISTRICTS AND FIRE PROTECTION DISTRICTS

Under New York State Law, fire districts have the legal status of "district corporations." Because fire districts may contract debt and require the municipalities within which they exist to levy taxes on their behalf, they are independent units of local government.

Cities and villages may have fire departments which provide fire protection for their residents. Towns, however, have no authority to provide fire protection as a town service, although they may create the position of fire marshal to inspect schools, hospitals, and other institutions and to grant permits for the storage of gasoline and chemicals.

Historically in towns, population was sparse and fires, while being catastrophic to the individuals concerned, were more a personal than a communal threat. Early fire protection came from neighbors forming bucket brigades. Following the bucket brigade came a loosely knit group which acquired some firefighting equipment. From this beginning sprang the modern-day volunteer fire companies.

For many years, volunteer fire companies supplied fire protection without governmental assistance or support. Gradually, however, expanding town populations, the high cost of equipment, and the need to provide the volunteers with compensation, in case of duty-related death or injury, forced the independent fire services to look to government for help. In towns this was solved, not on a townwide basis, but through the establishment of districts on an area-by-area basis. These districts took two differing forms: fire districts and fire protection districts.

Fire Districts

Like school districts, fire districts may have boundaries that cross town and even county lines. Residents of the over 800 fire districts in the state elect the governing body, a five member board of fire commissioners, one of whom is elected each year to a five year term. Elections are held in December. The board of fire commissioners operates under Section 176 of **New York State Town Law**.

A fire district is empowered by the state to determine its own budget and the town (or towns) in which it lies has no authority to change a fire district budget, as the district depends on the parent town(s) only for its creation and the collection of taxes to meet its needs. Fire districts have neither constitutional tax nor debt limits, but have strict statutory limitations on their finance authority.

The single purpose of a fire district's board of commissioners is to make provision for fire fighting within the district. To do so, the commissioners often establish their own fire department or company to do the actual fire fighting. In other cases, particularly in rural areas, the commissioners of a fire district may contract with a neighboring village or fire district for service rather than setting up their own department.

Fire Protection Districts

Fire protection districts, on the other hand, are quite different from fire districts as they are not separate from town government. Over 1000 fire protection districts have been set up by town governments for the purpose of providing fire protection by contract, usually with a nearby village or a neighboring fire district for fire fighting services. The town board serves as the governing body of a fire protection district, as it does for a water district or a street lighting district.

IMPROVEMENT DISTRICTS

When part of a county or town requires a service not otherwise provided for, that county or town may create a special district within which the service may be administered and financed. Units of local government may join together to serve some of the residents of each and charge back to those residents each unit's share of the cost. Among the services provided are water, sewage, sewage disposal, refuse and garbage disposal, snow removal, sidewalks, public parking, parks, libraries, and public docks.

There are over 5000 special districts in the state. Of these about 800 are fire districts which are the only ones to be regarded as local government units because of their independent power to contract debt and levy taxes. Taxes may be raised and debt incurred on behalf of other districts by the municipalities in which they lie. Since 1932, the creation of special districts with independent boards has been forbidden. Only a few, mostly on Long Island, are still administered by independent boards of commissioners rather than by town officials.

County Improvement Districts

A county improvement district may be created under **New York State County Law** to provide water, sewer, drainage, or refuse disposal service to part of a county. These districts are used increasingly in the state to broaden a service area beyond the boundaries of a single municipality without covering the entire county. Charges for the service provided are paid by those who receive the benefits, without imposing financial obligations upon taxpayers outside the area served.

Town Improvement Districts

When part of a town requires a service not otherwise provided for, the town may create a special district under New York State Town Law within which the service may be administered and financed. There are over 6000 special town improvement districts in the New York State. These districts are not considered local governments because they do not exist independently of the towns which form them. Their budgets are approved by the town board, whose members serve as commissioners of the district.

The largest number of districts provide drainage, fire protection, street lighting, sanitary sewers, and water; although services that can be provided by improvement districts include ambulance, street curbing, health services, and public parking, among others.

Revenues for many special improvement districts come from property taxes although some districts are financed by either a unit charge or a formula based on acreage, front footage, water use, or some other factor.

PUBLIC AUTHORITIES

The public authority is another mechanism by which a specific service may be provided. Authorities are classified as public benefit corporations, and each is created for a specific purpose, such as the provision of water, sewage service, housing, or parking facilities. They are established by action of the state legislature.

Authorities commonly are established within a city or a county to provide a service such as housing. Regional authorities, such as those providing transportation services often encompass several counties. Chapter 6 discusses how these authorities are financed.

PART III

SERVICES TO STATE RESIDENTS

The people of New York State receive a broad range of services from the state government. Of these, the state's role in education, welfare, health, mental health and environmental protection deserve particular attention because, in one way or another, they affect the lives of most citizens. These services account for more than 70 percent of the state's total expenditures, and their quality and cost is a matter of intense public interest.

Responsibility for providing these services is now shared by state and local governments. The dual basis of finance and supervision is intended to keep important functions of government close to the people while insuring uniform, minimum standards of service across the state. However, expanding concepts of the obligations of government to its citizens have encouraged huge expenditures by localities as well as by the state.

Local governments have protested vigorously the fiscal burdens of state mandated standards and programs and have pressured the state, with its broader revenue base, to assume a growing share of the costs.

At the same time, localities have tried to retain a voice in policies governing the delivery of services. Tension and conflict over responsibility for providing these services and for funding them are likely to mold state-local relationships for some time to come.

CHAPTER 9
EDUCATION IN NEW YORK STATE

New York's largest single public expenditure is for education; the average level of its per pupil spending in the elementary and secondary schools is among the highest in the nation. New York operates the nation's largest state university system and aids the great majority of its college students either through direct tuition grants or through direct support to the educational institutions they attend.

The greater share of funding the cost of elementary and secondary school education has fallen on the 734 local school districts, which range from small elementary school districts of only a few hundred children to the "Big Five" cities of New York City, Buffalo, Syracuse, Rochester, and Yonkers. Districts vary in the amount of property wealth and income wealth behind each student. Some districts possess large industrial and business wealth; others must rely only on the taxes paid by home owners. Within broad state standards, the programs and finances of each school district have traditionally reflected its constituency's character, needs, and willingness and ability to support education.

All local districts are subject to a variety of external forces. In response to recent changes in the patterns of families, the role of women, and the national economy, schools are asked to help solve such diverse problems as the growing number of teenage pregnancies, the needs of single-parent families, drugs, Acquired Immunodeficiency Syndrome (AIDS), and the education of the homeless. Government and the private sector have criticized the educational establishment for what they see as a failure to educate our children to function adequately in today's marketplace. National studies have called for far-reaching reform. One New York State study after another has demanded reform in the funding and delivery of education. These have included reports by the Fleischmann and Ruben Commissions; the most recent is the Temporary State Commission on the Distribution of State Aid to Local School Districts. Presently, schools and the state are responding to demands that teachers have a greater role in the management of schools.

Districts are also squeezed by the need to repair or replace aging facilities after years of neglect during the inflationary years of the 1970s and 1980s. Most of these facilities contain asbestos, now known to be hazardous to health, and which must be removed or contained; the cost can be staggering. Districts must respond to the spiraling costs of health and liability insurance, of meeting the needs of the disabled and those students with English as a Second Language (ESL, now referred to as English for Speakers of Other Languages), of funding new regents requirements including the Regents Action Plan, and of replacing educational materials annually. Finally, districts face the challenge of an aging teacher population eligible for retirement and a shortage of new teachers. Because local tax resources have not expanded sufficiently to support these burgeoning demands, local school systems in New York State are looking to the state for greater financial assistance (see Figure 9-1).

FINANCING EDUCATION

Except in the big cities, school districts are separate units of local government with independent power to tax and to spend public money. They raise revenue to support their schools through a local property tax; in the largest cities, education costs are paid out of general city funds. Public revenues also fund health services, textbooks, transportation, and certain other programs offered in all nonpublic schools. Over half the money spent on elementary and secondary education in New York State comes from local revenue sources.

All school districts in New York State receive financial assistance from the state in several major areas, the largest of which is operating aid. This aid is allocated to school districts using a formula established by the legislature. The share each district receives is determined by the local real property wealth and income wealth behind each pupil attending its public schools. The state sets a ceiling on the amount it will contribute to each district's expenditures. Although this ceiling has been raised often, the raises have not kept pace with local expenses. The state's aid formula has also been amended from time to time to take into account special expenses including needs associated with transportation, costs of educating the handicapped, payment for construction of buildings and playgrounds, and combatting the special problems of poverty. Some aid has been weighted to help big city school districts and the special needs of their

104

SCHOOL ADMINISTRATION ON THE LOCAL LEVEL
MAJOR TYPES OF SCHOOL DISTRICTS IN NEW YORK STATE

	COMMON SCHOOL DISTRICTS	UNION FREE SCHOOL DISTRICTS	CENTRAL SCHOOL DISTRICTS (ALSO CONSOLIDATED)	CITY SCHOOL DISTRICTS and ENLARGED CITY SCHOOL DISTRICTS — Population over 125,000	CITY SCHOOL DISTRICTS and ENLARGED CITY SCHOOL DISTRICTS — Population under 125,000
DEFINITION	Limited to operation of elementary schools. Of 19 such districts in 1988, 14 operated schools. The balance contracted with other districts for the education of their children.	Authorized to operate junior and senior high schools as well as elementary schools. 175 in 1988.	Formed by combining existing districts to provide better facilities and larger areas for taxation and administration. 478 in 1988.	Buffalo, New York City, Rochester, Syracuse and Yonkers.	Wholly or partly within a city of less than 125,000. May combine with adjoining Union Free or Common School Districts to pool resources of the larger area. 57 in 1988.
BOARD OF EDUCATION				N.Y.C.: NYC governed by special statutory provision for 32 semi-autonomous elected local boards and a central board responsible for high school and other designated functions. Others: 3 to 9 members, four to six year terms. Three cities elect boards; two have mayoral appointees.	
Size	1 or 3 trustees	3 to 9 trustees	5, 7 or 9 trustees		5, 7 or 9 members
Term	Three year terms	Three or five year terms	Three or five year terms		Five year terms
How Selected	Elected	Elected	Elected		Elected; however, in one city they are appointed by the Mayor.
ADMINISTRATION	Superintendent appointed by the Board of Education, by contract; serves at pleasure of the board.				
BUDGET	Must be voted on each year by voters. Boards unable to achieve approval of the budget at district elections are authorized to operate schools under austerity programs. Decision may be made at an annual meeting held on any Tuesday between May 1 and June 30. If school district is divided into election districts and if voting machines are used, a district need only schedule a public hearing to discuss the expenditures of funds and the budget. The hearing must be scheduled not more than 30 nor less than 10 days before the budget vote is to take place.			Part of a total city budget adopted by the City Council.	Adopted by board after a hearing.
ELECTIONS	At Annual Meeting or on day designated for public vote (see above), usually in the spring. Nominations by petition with minimum of 25 signatures. Absentee voting for school board members only, at local option, in districts having personal registration.			New York City Central School Board, Yonkers and Rensselaer have appointed boards. Elections are scheduled in May or June, except Rochester and Syracuse vote in November.	1st Tuesday in May, General and special registration. Nominations by petition with minimum of 100 signatures.
TRANSPORTATION	Required for all public, private or parochial school students: K-8, living 2-15 miles from school; those in grades 9-12, 3-15 miles. Changes may be made at the option of the local Board, but state aid is paid only for 2-15 miles. Districts must provide door to door transportation for handicapped students between ages 5-21, within 50 miles radius. Districts receive 90% state reimbursement for transportation costs incurred the previous year.			Optional at discretion to School Board to any grade level or all. If provided, must include equivalent service to public, private and parochial students. Mileage requirements same as for preceding districts.	

Figure 9-1

pupils. Other needs of school districts are addressed by separate forms of assistance including high tax aid, supplemental support aid, and categorical aid.

For many years, about 40 percent of per pupil costs were borne by the state. By 1988, the state's share had risen to 44 percent; the portion paid by state funds totalling almost $8 billion (for approximately three million school children). This amount represents the total portion for the entire state. Individual districts actually receive from under 10 percent to a high over 80 percent of their educational costs. State support for capital construction ranges from no support to over 90%.

The major thrust of the state's school aid has been to equalize educational expenditures and tax effort. However, doing so has proved to be a difficult task involving measuring local wealth and costs, responding to the special needs of the cities, and at the same time, taking into account regional cost differences. The state gives a minimum "flat grant" to all districts, regardless of wealth. This grant ($360 per pupil) has remained the same since 1977. In addition, the legislature has continued to support "save harmless," a policy that guarantees that a district will receive the same aid it received the previous year.

For a number of years, the governor and regents have proposed to eliminate flat grants and save harmless. However, school districts that would lose funds have argued that all districts are entitled to some return for education on their tax dollar, and have joined together to protect the formula that assures their aid. The legislators, reflecting their own constituencies, have tended to compromise, changing the operating aid formulas as little as possible but increasing the total educational appropriation by adding as many as 42 special (categorical) aid formulas. In addition to the exceptions in the formula, the equitable allocation of state aid is complicated by real property being assessed on a different basis in each community. The result is a great difference from district to district in school tax rates and in the amount spent per pupil.

Each year finds the state legislature balancing the proposals for aid submitted by the Board of Regents, the governor, its own members, and the Educational Conference Board, a consortium whose component organizations include the school teacher union, superintendents, business officials, school board members, administrators, Parent-Teacher Associations (PTAs), and the Public Education Association.

STATE STRUCTURE OF EDUCATION

Virtually all approved educational facilities in the state come under the umbrella of the University of the State of New York established in 1984. Its purpose, under direction of the Board of Regents, is to promote the development of educational facilities and to establish and enforce educational and performance standards across the state. Under the purview of the university, all public, private, and parochial schools; institutions of higher education; all libraries, museums, and educational and cultural organizations admitted to or incorporated by the university.

THE BOARD OF REGENTS

Sixteen regents serve on the Board of Regents, one from each judicial district and four from the state at large. Each is elected by the legislature for a seven year term. In recent years, as the regents have become involved in such controversial issues as appropriate programs for children and "youth at risk" and provisions for educational and fiscal accountability, the election of members of the Board of Regents has taken place in a highly political setting.

The regents appoint the President of the University of the State of New York, more generally known by the title the Commissioner of Education. The commissioner serves at the pleasure of the regents and heads the State Department of Education, which is the regents' administrative agency.

In overseeing education in the state, the regents charter, register and inspect educational institutions; establish and stimulate education extension work; conduct exams, confer degrees, and grant credentials. They supervise requirements for admission to a broad range of vocations and to all professions except law, and they set licensing standards for both businesses and professions. One of their tasks is to define the needs and goals of education to the governor, to the legislature, and to the people of the state. Their voice is one of many on this subject.

DEPARTMENT OF EDUCATION

Under the general supervision of the commissioner, the department administers the educational policies of the state. It provides teachers and school administrators with advisory services on curricula and all areas of school management. The commissioner has quasijudicial as well as executive power which includes power to hear appeals in matters involving the educational community and questions on codes or rules adopted in an individual school.

STATE-LOCAL RELATIONSHIPS

Within the state structure, local and city school boards have day-to-day responsibility for administering public education in New York State. All elementary and secondary schools are organized into school districts whose governing bodies are elected boards of education, except in some cities that have appointed boards.

These boards are actually agencies of the state, responsible to the Board of Regents and subject to policies mandated by the legislature. Legislative action affects employment policies for teachers, governs school election procedures, and defines the jurisdiction of boards of education in other ways. For organization of education in New York City, see Chapter 7--New York City section.

BOCES

Boards of Cooperative Education Services (BOCES) are regional collaboratives, originated by an act of the New York State Legislature over 40 years ago, that provide a wide range of educational programs and services to serve the mutual educational needs of local school districts. In 1988 there were 41 BOCES in New York.

Originally focused primarily on vocational education, BOCES' broad array of services now include the following programs:

• instructional programs in the areas of special education for students with many different disabilities
• occupational education programs for secondary level students

- adult education, including upgrading and retraining programs, high school equivalency preparation, English for Speakers of Other Languages, and workplace literacy
- alternative educational programs for high school students who have been unsuccessful in traditional schools settings
- advanced placement and advanced level courses for students who are gifted/talented
- advanced art programs to talented high school students
- staff and professional development programs for teachers and administrators
- managerial and instructional technology support services
- and student transportation services, transportation safety training, field trip services and school bus maintenance services.

Members of the BOCES boards are elected by the boards of education of the member school districts. The administrative officer is a district superintendent.

STATE UNIVERSITY OF NEW YORK (SUNY) SYSTEM

The State University of New York (SUNY) is only one of the constituents of the University of the State of New York. Before 1948, the State University consisted only of a handful of programs funded on the campuses of private colleges and universities in the state. With the upsurge in college enrollment after World War II, the state embarked on a massive construction program to establish an independent state university. Today, it is the nation's largest system of higher education. Its campuses now include four university centers, two medical centers, 13 colleges of arts and science, five specialized colleges, six two-year agricultural and technical colleges, 30 locally sponsored community colleges, and four health science centers.

In the fall of 1987, SUNY had more than 30,000 full- and part-time instructors and an enrollment of nearly 370,000 credit students at 64 campuses, outstripping admission rates to New York's private colleges. In 1979, the state took over the full cost of senior colleges of the City University of New York (CUNY). It gave CUNY campuses equivalent standing and financing with other New York State colleges under the state university system. In the fall of 1988, CUNY enrolled approximately 103,000 full time and 85,000 part-time students.

CHAPTER 10
SOCIAL AND HUMAN SERVICES

The care of those in need has been a public responsibility in our country for three centuries. Our concept of this responsibility has expanded gradually over the years to include children in many categories of need and others who have become dependent through unemployment, accidents, old age, illness, blindness or other disability, or through the death of the family breadwinner. The goal of the New York State Department of Social Services is to ensure that dependent or disabled persons receive financial and medical assistance or other supportive services necessary to achieve the greatest degree of independence possible.

The Department of Social Services has basic responsibility not only for income assistance programs but for day care and all aspects of child welfare including neglected and abused children, adoption, and foster care. Its services for adults include protective services, senior centers, programs for displaced homemakers, services to abused wives, and family planning counselling.

The department is headed by a commissioner appointed by the governor with the advice and consent of the Senate. The department is organized into eight program divisions and four support offices that have primary responsibility for administration; establishing programs, setting policies and regulations, and implementing state and federal mandates.

Locally, social services are administered through 58 social service districts found in every county and in New York City. These social service districts are headed by local commissioners who operate local programs and administer state programs under directives and standards of the New York State Department of Social Services.

Public assistance falls into two major categories: delivery of services and delivery of money. The former includes help for families, children and individuals, and is not limited to those who receive cash assistance. It may come from agencies other than the state Department of Social Serv-

ices. Housing relocation, counseling, mental hygiene, day care, employment training, and supportive services to the elderly are examples of such
services.

Programs that carry cash benefits are generally designated as income
maintenance. They include Aid to Families with Dependent Children
(AFDC); Home Relief (HR); and Supplemental Security Income (SSI) for
the aged, blind and disabled. In addition, the medical assistance program
(Medicaid) provides cash payment to those providing medical services
and nursing home care for the needy; and the Food Stamp Program provides cash assistance in the form of nonnegotiable food purchase coupons.

A complex web of intergovernmental financing supports these programs, and the mix may be different for each program. This complicates
their administration, but each program can be understood by who administers and delivers the cash payments, who is the source of the money, and
who is responsible for identifying those eligible to receive it.

In 1987-88 the state disbursed nearly $125 billion in public assistance
and medical assistance. The federal government pays 50 percent of the
cost of Medicaid and AFDC, with the state and localities sharing equally
in the remainder. Home Relief is funded half by the state and half by local
governments. Food stamps and SSI are fully funded at the federal level
although New York adds a state supplement to the SSI payment. In New
York State, all income maintenance programs are administered through
the Department of Social Services, except SSI, which comes under the
jurisdiction of the Social Security Administration. The number of programs and the amounts expended for them, however, do not measure the
level of assistance to the recipient. This is determined by two factors: the
standard of need and the schedule of allowance to meet that need. As a
general rule, the administrative agencies (either the U.S. Department of
Health and Human Services or the state's department of Social Services)
defines the level of need. It is up to the appropriate legislative body, either
Congress or the New York State Legislature, to determine how much of
the need will be met.

During the 1980s, the federal government withdrew support of many
social benefit programs. As a result, New York State has attempted to
increase its commitment to those in need. In recent years, special emphasis

has been placed on the homeless, disabled needy adults, and children. A number of pilot programs have been established to assist pregnant teenagers. Emphasis has also been placed on preparing clients — including mothers of very young children — to support themselves and their families through training and employment programs. These programs often include transitional support services such as transportation, health care benefits, and day care.

The Department of Social Services has created a unit to supervise and regulate licensed day care as well as to increase the supply of quality day care in New York State.

The Homeless Housing and Assistance Program (HHAP) was developed in 1983 and provides grants to support the capital cost of projects designed to expand and improve housing and shelter for the state's homeless population.

HEALTH

The New York State Department of Health is responsible for safeguarding the health of New York's residents. To accomplish this effectively, the department is organized into two major program units: the Office of Public Health and the Office of Health Systems Management. The total budget for the department in 1987-88 was $758 million.

The Office of Public Health (OPH) is responsible for preserving the health of New York State's residents through education, research, and prevention of accidents and diseases. Many of the programs administered by OPH are aimed at enhancing child growth and development through early prenatal care, newborn screening, supplemental foods for pregnant women and children, immunization, school health programs, and teen counseling. Other activities focus on occupational health hazards and the potential health threat of toxic contaminants in our environment. Still others are geared toward combatting communicable diseases through continued monitoring of drinking water purity and restaurant sanitation, and through follow-up investigation of hospital infections and sexually transmitted disease cases.

Research is a major function of the Office of Public Health. Clinical, laboratory, and epidemiological studies are focused on such public health problems as birth defects, kidney disease, health manpower needs, toxic effects of chemical substances and radiation, sexually transmitted diseases, and cancer. Other research efforts aim to improve laboratory testing methods, expand our understanding of the body's basic biosystems, or reverse deterioration of our lakes and streams.

The Office of Public Health monitors the need for skilled health professionals throughout the state and identifies underserved areas for training support programs. It also oversees the medical conduct of physicians and takes disciplinary action against individuals who violate the law. Finally, OPH is responsible for maintaining records of every birth, death, marriage, and divorce that occurs in the state, and for protecting the confidentiality of those records.

The Office of Health Systems Management (OHSM) is responsible for assuring that quality medical care is available to all New York State residents regardless of where they live or their ability to pay. The Department of Health, through OHSM, has direct authority over all health care institutions in the state covered by the Public Health Law, including hospitals, nursing homes, diagnostic and treatment centers, and many home care providers. To protect the welfare of patients, the state certifies all health care institutions and sets standards governing nearly every aspect of health facility operation.

Ensuring that limited health care dollars are prudently spent and administering programs to keep the cost of health care services within affordable limits are other primary goals of OHSM. The Office of Health Systems Management develops reimbursement methods and sets the rate each health facility will be paid for services to patients covered by Medicaid. Those rates form the basis for Medicare, Blue Cross, Workers' Compensation, and no-fault insurance rates. OHSM also audits health facility costs and charges and reviews the financial implications of health facility construction and expansion. Finally, OHSM is responsible for statewide planning to assure that state health care resources are efficiently allocated.

The Department of Health operates three specialized research and patient care institutions: Roswell Park Memorial Institute, a comprehensive cancer center in Buffalo; Helen Hayes Hospital in West Haverstraw which specializes in treatment of physical disabilities; and the New York State Veterans' Home in Oxford, a residential health care facility for veterans and their dependents. These institutions also serve as statewide resources for the training of health professionals and dissemination of preventive health information to New York State residents.

MENTAL HYGIENE

There are four agencies responsible for mental hygiene: the Office of Mental Health; the Office of Mental Retardation and Developmental Disabilities; the Division of Alcoholism and Alcohol Abuse; and the Division of Substance Abuse Services.

In 1988, several major new programs were underway in the Office of Mental Health. A new intensive care management program staffed by highly-trained mental health professionals will help serious and persistently mentally ill people during crises and find needed residential and treatment services. Five hundred case managers, with a low staff to client ratio, will be trained to serve these cases. In addition, a community development program is being undertaken to develop alternative residential beds and supportive services for the mentally ill in the community. As of 1988, a statewide total of 5200 beds were available, of which 1300 were in New York City alone. The ultimate goal is 13,000 beds by 1996. Supportive employment and vocational rehabilitation programs will result in employment opportunities in 1989 for over 5000 contract services. Services to the homeless mentally ill in New York City include a special 50-bed extended-care unit located at Creedmoor Psychiatric Center.

The average daily census of the psychiatric centers dropped from 19,901 to 18,300 during fiscal year 1987-88 due to development of community residential and treatment program alternatives. The office maintains 31 facilities, of which 30 are accredited by the Joint Commission on Accreditation of Health Care Organizations. The total state 1986 mental health budget was $1.7 million.

The Office of Mental Retardation and Developmental Disabilities (OMRDD) is mandated to assure the development of comprehensive plans, programs, and services in the areas of research, prevention, care, treatment, rehabilitation, and education and training of persons with mental retardation and developmental disabilities.

In 1988 there were fewer than 8300 individuals in state developmental centers. Over 19,000 individuals reside in a comprehensive range of community residential settings, including supportive apartments, supervised community residences, family care, and intermediate care facilities for the developmentally disabled. As a matter of policy, placement of individuals into community residential settings from developmental centers is conditional upon the availability of appropriate day and support services. These services include education programs under the auspices of the New York State Department of Education, day-treatment programs which accommodate substantially impaired individuals, day-training programs which provide transitional training of individuals moving toward independence, and comprehensive vocational rehabilitation services, sheltered workshops, and supported work programs for those individuals capable of a greater degree of independent action. Supporting this system are ancillary networks of transportation, recreation, and social services.

As of April 1, 1988, OMRDD certified 892 voluntary operated (private, not-for-profit) community residences serving over 5300 individuals and 570 voluntary operated intermediate care facilities for the developmentally disabled with space for over 5800 people. The state also certified voluntary operated day activities for over 36,000 individuals in more than 380 distinct locations. These include 143 day training/sheltered workshop programs serving 2005 people and 127 day treatment programs serving 12,188 people.

The Division of Alcoholism and Alcohol Abuse is responsible for planning, developing, coordinating, and evaluating a comprehensive system of services to alcoholic persons, alcohol abusers, and their families. The division also educates the public about the disease of alcoholism, and the risks associated with alcohol use, and it conducts research into the causes and treatment of the problem.

In 1988, there were approximately 1.2 million "problem drinkers" in New York State, close to half a million of New York State's children lived in alcoholic families, and about 16.5 percent of New Yorkers over age 16 described themselves as the child of at least one alcoholic parent. Such children are at high risk of developing alcoholism. Treatment programs have grown substantially in recent years but are still meeting only about ten percent of the need. Alcohol abuse costs an estimated $8 billion to $10 billion per year in health care, lost productivity and employment, insurance claims, and fatal accidents.

The division has 650 employees across the state in its central and regional offices, 13 state-operated rehabilitation centers, and the Research Institute on Alcoholism in Buffalo. The 13 alcoholism treatment centers have 540 beds and provide over 200,000 days of medical, psychological, vocational, and other services to 5000 individual clients each year. The typical length of treatment is four to six weeks. On any given day in 1988 there were 32,000 persons in outpatient programs; 13,000 in alcohol crisis centers for detoxification; 1300 in state-operated and private rehabilitation centers; and 600 in community residences (halfway houses).

The Division of Substance Abuse Services has programs of prevention, treatment, research, and training for substance abuse problems. During 1986 and 1987, substance abuse continued to be one of the leading threats to the health and well-being of New York State residents. More than six million persons, some 44 percent of the state's population, had used a substance nonmedically in their lifetimes. About half of those had used substances recently (within a six month period, as estimated in a research study). Of recent users, about half were considered to be "regular" users (approximately once a week), and one-fourth were "heavy" abusers (almost daily). In all, there were more than 616,000 heavy abusers of nonnarcotics and 260,000 heavy abusers of narcotic drugs.

The major developments of 1986 and 1987 were the continued escalation in the abuse of cocaine, particularly in the form known as "crack," and the growing intensity of the AIDS epidemic among intravenous drug users. In 1986, there were 12,586 admissions to funded drug-free programs with cocaine as the primary drug of abuse. Between 1986 and 1987, the number of cocaine admissions climbed to 15,984. Between April 1986 and March 1987, the number of AIDS cases in New York State increased from 7211 to 11,008. Of these, fully one-third were known to be intravenous drug users. Projections are that as many as 50 to 60 percent of intravenous drug users had been exposed to the human immunodeficiency virus (HIV) associated with AIDS.

Programs sponsored by the division include school and community based prevention; "Crack Down on Crack" rallies; project LEARN (Law Enforcement Awareness Resource Network), which seeks to augment the traditional "supply reduction" activities of law enforcement with a "demand reduction" focus, by providing training and technical assistance directly to police personnel; methadone programs; AIDS initiatives; homeless services programs; and criminal justice initiatives. The 1987-88 agency budget was $162 million.

LABOR

Of all the state's activities in providing services and regulating business and government, nowhere does it have a more pervasive impact than in the field of labor. There its policies affect almost everyone. In general, the state's labor activities, administered by the Department of Labor, fall into three categories:

- protection of wages, hours, and working conditions
- services to the unemployed, the underemployed and the disabled
- the conduct of labor relations between employers and employees.

The state Department of Labor is chiefly responsible for these functions. In addition, the Department of Civil Service serves as central personnel agency for state offices; and the Public Employee Relations Board (PERB) carries out state labor policies through its role in resolving disputes between state and local governments and their employees.

The Labor Department is headed by a Commissioner of Labor who is appointed by and reports directly to the governor. Both the civil service department and PERB are headed by commissions, whose three members are appointed by the governor, with the consent of the Senate, for six-year terms. In each case, the governor is barred from naming more than two of the three from the same political party and is empowered to designate one of the three as chairman.

Wages and Working Conditions

Perhaps the most encompassing labor standard in the state is that governing the minimum wage. Today only a few professionals, executives, independent salesmen, taxidrivers, students obtaining vocational experience, and churchmen are exempted from its provisions. Farm labor comes under separate protective wage policies of the state.

These policies are administered by the department's Division of Labor Standards, which not only enforces minimum wages but strictly regulates hours of employment and working conditions for minors. The division also carries out inspections and investigates complaints relating to farm and home work establishments. A separate law provides for payment of the prevailing wage rate for those engaged in construction projects for any governmental agency.

The labor department is also responsible for supervising health and safety standards affecting the general public. The department administers the **Public Employees Safety and Health Act**, and inspects places of public assembly, boilers, amusement parks and ski tows. The federal **Occupational Safety and Health Act (OSHA)** provides enforcement of safety and health standards in private industry. State safety laws not covered by OSHA are enforced by the New York State Labor Department.

Work Force Services

New York State's employment services operate through a statewide local office network of the Department of Labor's Job Services. These act as placement agencies for skilled, unskilled, and professional job seekers.

The most widely used of the labor department's services is unemployment insurance, which provides weekly benefits for up to six months (and longer in periods of high unemployment) to almost everyone except domestic workers earning less than $500 a year, part time student workers, farm workers and the self-employed. Unemployment insurance payments are financed by an employer-paid payroll tax which varies according to a company's past employment and unemployment experience.

The state also administers the **Workers' Compensation Law,**which provides cash benefits and cost of medical treatment, including rehabilitation, to eligible workers temporarily disabled because of work-related injury or disease. The dependents or the spouse of a worker who dies from such an injury or illness may also receive cash benefits. The amount of the benefit claim is determined by a panel of the Workers' Compensation Board, a body of 13 members appointed by the governor and confirmed by the Senate for seven-year terms.

In addition, the state requires most employers to carry coverage under its Disability Benefits Program which provides for cash payments to eligible employees who are temporarily disabled by illnesses or accidents that are not job related. In 1977, the legislature also authorized these cash payments as replacement for earnings lost because of pregnancy. Benefits under this program are paid by self-insured employers or their insurance carriers.

The state participates in a number of employability development and on-the-job training programs, funded almost entirely by the federal government. Among these are the **Job Training Partnership Act (JTPA)** in which the state acts as the administrator for local service delivery areas (SDAs) in this federal program. **The Comprehensive Employment Training Act (CETA)** provides jobs and training in public service, as well as placements in the private sector. The Department of Labor also administers the Displaced Homemaker Program and other state-funded training programs, most of them targeted toward youth.

A program designed in the mid-1970s to reduce the welfare rolls makes the Department of Labor responsible for placement services for employable welfare recipients other than those in the Federal Work Incentive Program. The state's purpose is to expose welfare recipients to placement, training and counseling services, which are largely funded by the federal government. A few, including the Affirmative Action Program, the Civil Services Career Development Program and the Urban Center Program, are state financed.

Since 1945, New York State has had a Division of Human Rights whose responsibilities include elimination and prevention of discrimination in employment as well as in housing and in places of public accommodation. Over the years. the statute defining the division's powers has often been amended to broaden its scope. Within the past decade the division has focused on policies to promote minority participation in on-the-job training programs, employment in publicly subsidized construction, admission to labor unions, and increasingly to end practices that discriminate against women.

The division may generally adopt and promulgate rules and regulations, and investigate and pass on complaints alleging discrimination in employment in labor unions or in training programs on the basis of race, creed, color, national origin or sex.

The work of the division has frequently been beset by complexities involving minorities demanding larger quotas of jobs on publicly subsidized construction; contractors who blame unions for inadequate numbers of qualified minority workers; unions blaming contractors for inadequate on-the-job training opportunities; and the conflicting interests of the state in timely completion of public works projects under conditions of fair employment.

The human rights division is headed by a commissioner appointed by the governor with the consent of the Senate. Decisions of the division may be appealed to the New York State Human Rights Appeal Board, which consists of four members appointed by the governor, with the consent of the Senate, for six year terms.

LABOR RELATIONS

The state's **Labor Relations Act** governs relations between employers and their employees, guaranteeing workers the right to bargain collectively through representatives of their own choosing. The New York State Labor Relations Board administers this law and investigates complaints that rights of labor or management have been violated. The board is empowered to enforce the act through orders that may, for example, reinstate a discharged employee or mandate a company to bargain with an employee organization.

Like the labor relations board, the State Mediation Board consists of three members appointed by the governor, with the consent of the Senate, for six-year terms. Its function is to provide voluntary mediation services to the parties in a labor dispute. If the dispute affects the public interest and cannot be settled by mediation, the Commissioner of Labor may appoint a Board of Inquiry to hold public and private hearings, subpoena witnesses and take evidence, and publish a report of its findings, thus bringing pressure to bear on the parties.

Labor relations for public employees are governed by the **Taylor Law**, enacted in 1967, to settle disputes between any state or local governmental agency and its employees. The law outlaws strikes, and establishes a schedule of penalties that includes fines and jail sentences for violations. The Taylor Law provides for procedures for conducting contract negotiations, and the Public Employees Relations Board, which mediates when the parties to a dispute are at an impasse. The most far-reaching effect of the Taylor Law is to establish the right of public employees to organize into unions and to bargain collectively.

In 1974, the Taylor Law was amended to require, for a trial period, binding arbitration in labor disputes between local governments and police and firefighters' unions. Since then the legislature, at the urging of the unions, has extended the effect of the amendment. However, local government officials who argue that contracts financed through tax revenues should not be determined by arbitrators who are not responsible to the taxpayers.

HOUSING

The lack of affordable housing has been addressed for 60 years by the state government beginning with the **Housing Law** of 1926, which established the New York State Board of Housing. The Division of Housing and Community Renewal (DHCR) has two major functions: it assists in the production and preservation of low- and moderate-income housing; affordable housing; and it administers the rent-regulation system as it affects New York City. The DHCR was operated under the direction of the commissioner of the division who was appointed by the governor and approved by the Senate. In 1985, the commissioner was appointed to the additional post of Director of Housing and became responsible for all housing activities in New York State including the State of New York Mortgage Agency (SONYMA) and the New York State Housing Finance Agency (HFA). In early 1988 the position of Commissioner of DHCR/

Director of Housing became vacant. Later that year, the governor appointed a seven-member Housing Task Force to make recommendations on the state's overall housing policy. Administrative changes were planned for 1989 based on the task force report.

Affordable housing has been provided to more than 175,000 low and middle income families in more than 400 housing developments built under programs administered by DHCR. Since 1939, New York has financed and constructed 66,123 apartments for low income families in 143 projects owned and operated by 42 municipal housing authorities. The projects are financed by $960 million in general obligation bond authorizations and are subsidized with $42 million. The state subsidy reduces rent for apartments by meeting the difference between rental income and operating costs. However, these operating costs have risen faster than the tenants' ability to pay and have eroded reserve funds necessary to pay for upgrading and replacing older projects. As a result, DHCR has assisted housing authorities in upgrading their developments through the Federal Public Housing Acquisition Program and New York State Modernization Program.

Other innovations in housing include the Low Income Housing Trust Fund Program, established in 1985, which administers the disbursement of $25 million to stimulate the development of affordable housing for low income persons by rehabilitating or converting underutilized or vacant buildings. A number of other programs, including the Housing Development Fund, provide incentives or loans for private sector individuals or not-for-profit groups to perform housing preservation and community renewal activities. Many of these programs exist because of massive federal cutbacks in the area of housing in the 1980s.

CHAPTER 11
ENVIRONMENT AND PUBLIC SERVICES

ENVIRONMENTAL CONSERVATION

Stewardship of the lands and waters of New York State has been a state responsibility since the first State Constitution, but the nature and extent of that responsibility has expanded enormously in the last 20 years. By 1969, growing public concern for the environment led to constitutional changes giving the legislature new authority to protect the state's natural resources.

In 1970, the Department of Environmental Conservation (DEC) was reorganized, consolidating particular functions of the Department of Health and the existing Environmental Conservation Department (fish and wildlife) into a single agency mandated to protect and enhance our natural environment.

Two major areas of responsibility were outlined: environmental quality and natural resources management. Environmental quality includes pollution control for air, water, and land, and hazardous and solid waste management. Natural resources management addresses protection and uses of our fish, wildlife, land, marine, and mineral resources.

In addition, DEC administers the **State Environmental Quality Review Act (SEQRA)**, which requires that environmental impact be considered before development or construction decisions are made.

Administration

A commissioner, appointed by the governor, directs the work of the DEC. The commissioner, who also serves as a member of the New York State Energy Planning Board, is charged with developing and monitoring the State Energy Master Plan. This board is directed to encourage energy conservation; to develop renewable energy sources such as solar heat, water, and wind; to promote energy production from solid waste; and to oversee prudent development of land-based and offshore deposits of natural gas and oil.

Central administration of the agency is conducted from its main office in Albany. There are nine regional offices and 19 suboffices which serve specific geographic areas. Regional offices provide numerous services including issuance of regulatory permits, technical and public education, assistance in the management of regional natural resources and enforcement of environmental laws and regulations (see Figures 11-1 and 11-2).

Environmental Quality

Environmental quality encompasses a variety of functions with an underlying goal of limiting the amounts and types of pollution discharged to air, land, or water.

The department establishes standards to measure air, land and water pollution. In conjunction with local and state health departments, it monitors and controls the release of polluting substances which may take the form of particulates, gases, dust, radiation, odors, liquids, nutrients, and thermal discharges.

AIR RESOURCES

In 1957, New York State enacted one of the nation's first air pollution control laws. For over 30 years, New York has operated a statewide air monitoring network. In 1985, New York again led the way by being the first state to issue regulations to reduce sulfur emissions specifically in response to the acid rain problem.

Regional offices regulated pollution limits for some 65,000 sources in 1988. Multiple contaminants including several toxic pollutants are sampled continuously at 150 stations statewide. The State Implementation Plan (SIP) guides New York's air management system to bring the state into compliance with federal air quality standards.

Implementation of air pollution control programs during the past 20 years has resulted in significantly improved air quality around the state. Concentrations of the six "criteria" contaminants (sulfur dioxide, carbon monoxide, ozone, lead, nitrogen oxides, and particulates) have steadily declined.

LEGEND
- Regional Headquarters
- Sub-Offices

REGION 6
State Office Building
317 Washington Street
Watertown, N.Y. 13601
(315) 785-2236

SUB-OFFICES
30 Court Street
Canton, N.Y. 13617
(315) 386-4546
State Office Building
207 Genesee Street
Utica, N.Y. 13503
(315) 793-2555
RD 3, Box 22A, Route 812
Lowville, N.Y. 13367
(315) 376-3521
225 N. Main Street
Herkimer, N.Y. 13350
(315) 866-6330

REGION 9
600 Delaware Avenue
Buffalo, N.Y. 14202
(716) 847-4600

SUB-OFFICES
215 South Work Street
Falconer, N.Y. 14733
(716) 665-6111
128 South Street
Olean, N.Y. 14760
(716) 372-0645

REGION 8
6274 E. Avon-Lima Road
Avon, N.Y. 14414
(716) 226-2466

SUB-OFFICE
115 Liberty Street
Bath, N.Y. 14810
(607) 776-2165
180 Clemans Ctr. Parkway
Elmira, N.Y. 14901
(607) 734-6289

REGION 7
7481 Henry Clay Blvd
Liverpool, N.Y. 13088
(315) 428-4497

SUB-OFFICES
PO Box 1169, Fisher Ave.
Cortland, N.Y. 13045
(607) 753-3095
Route 11
Kirkwood, N.Y. 13795
(607) 773-7763
Route 80
Sherburne, N.Y. 13460
(607) 674-2611

REGION 5
Route 86
Ray Brook, N.Y. 12977
(518) 891-8216

SUB-OFFICES
Box 220
Hudson Street Extension
Warrensburg, N.Y. 12885
(518) 623-3671
Main Street Extension
Northville, N.Y. 12134
(518) 863-4545

CENTRAL OFFICE
50 Wolf Road
Albany, N.Y. 12233-0001

REGION 4
2176 Guilderland Ave.
Schenectady, N.Y. 12306
(518) 382-0680

SUB-OFFICES
Route 10, Jefferson Road
Stamford, N.Y. 12167
(607) 652-7364
PO Box 430
Catskill, N.Y. 12414
(518) 943-4030 or 943-4394

REGION 3
21 South Putt Corners Road
New Paltz, N.Y. 12561
(914) 255-5453

SUB-OFFICE
202 Mamaroneck Ave.
White Plains, N.Y. 10601
(914) 761-6660

REGION 1
SUNY Campus
Building 40
Stony Brook, N.Y. 11794
(516) 751-7900

REGION 2
Hunters Point Plaza
47-40 21st Street
Long Island City, N.Y. 11101
(718) 482-4900

NEW YORK STATE DEPARTMENT OF
ENVIRONMENTAL CONSERVATION:
Regions and Suboffices

Figure 11-1

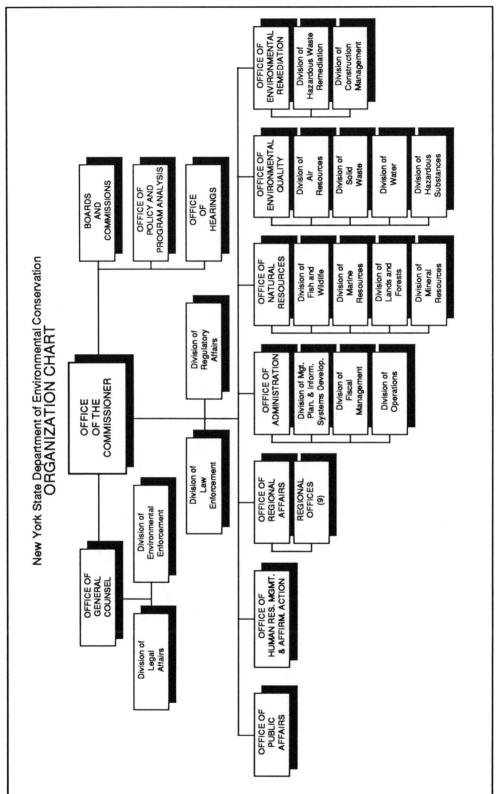

New York State Department of Environmental Conservation
ORGANIZATION CHART

Figure 11-2

WATER QUALITY AND QUANTITY

New York State has approximately 70,000 miles of streams and 4,000 lakes. More than one-third of the state's population receive their drinking water from groundwater. It is the responsibility of the Division of Water to maintain high quality and adequate quantity of our freshwater resources.

With one of the most comprehensive water pollution control permit programs in the country, the permits of the State Pollutant Discharge Elimination System (SPDES) specify which substances, and what amounts of these substances can be legally discharged into ground or surface waters. In 1987, the SPDES program regulated about 1600 major and minor discharges and some 5600 less significant discharges.

The Division of Water reviews the water quality classifications for over 450 streams, rivers, and lakes. There are five major classes of freshwater quality for New York State waters (see Figure 11-3).

Each water classification has its own set of water quality objectives and standards. Discharges into surface or groundwater must meet the standards for that particular water body.

Groundwater programs emphasize protection of aquifers (underground geologic formations that store and transmit significant quantities of ground water) from contamination. Three specific projects assist with prevention of further or future contamination of underground waters: 1) the groundwater mapping [locating] project; 2) the control programs for bulk storage of petroleum and hazardous substances; and 3) a spill response program for petroleum and hazardous substances. Chemical spills and leaks along with nonpoint source pollution are the principal threats to our ground and surface water quality.

Other water quality issues are managed in conjunction with the Division of Construction Management. These include wastewater facilities, flood control projects, and toxic and nutrient clean-up programs for lakes and rivers.

Focus on water quantity includes developing strategies for drought management and flow control. The goal of these programs is to ensure a sufficient water supply to support a wide range of usages across the state.

129

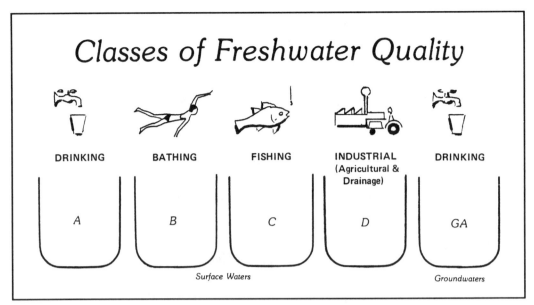

Figure 11-3

As part of the planning for adequate water supplies, the Division of Water is developing a Water Resources Strategy Program. The purpose of this program is to evaluate local water supplies and recommend improvements, such as water conservation, metering, or other use/management strategies. Controversial issues of intra/interstate water allocations, diversions, and releases will require new initiatives and increased attention to freshwater as a finite resource to be managed wisely.

SOLID AND HAZARDOUS WASTE

Regulating the reuse and disposal of all types of solid waste is the responsibility of three divisions: Hazardous Substances Regulation, Waste Remediation, and Solid Waste. These divisions oversee functions of active waste and chemical substances management and site remediation activities. Active waste management includes source reduction, recycling, resource recovery (the processing of solid waste for the purpose of converting it to energy or separating it for reuse) and safe disposal of solid waste. Remediation addresses clean-up and closure of past hazardous and solid waste sites.

Permits are issued to operators of landfills, resource recovery facilities and incinerators; and to transporters of hazardous wastes. In addition, a permit is required if a business stores, treats, or disposes of a specific quantity of hazardous waste.

Solid Waste. The beginning of statewide recycling began in 1982 with the **New York State Returnable Beverage Container Act,** commonly called the "Bottle Bill." This law requires a deposit on certain beverage containers (beer and carbonated soda) sold in the state. The deposit (five cents per container in 1988) is redeemed when the container is returned for reuse or recycling. The "Bottle Bill" has reduced the amount of solid waste to be landfilled or processed.

The New York Solid Waste Management Plan was presented to the governor and the legislature in 1987 by the DEC and was adopted in 1988. This plan establishes a hierarchy of methods for treatment of solid waste: source reduction, recycling, waste-to-energy and landfilling. To further the goals of this plan, DEC provides grants and technical assistance to localities sponsoring recycling and reuse programs.

Hazardous Substances. Approximately 2000 New York State industries generated hazardous waste in 1987. Some 200 additional facilities stored, treated, or disposed of regulated quantities of hazardous substances or wastes.

The Hazardous Substances Division permits and monitors these types of facilities, including transporters, to ensure that these hazardous substances or wastes are manifested, properly shipped and carefully handled en route to the disposal or recycling site.

The "manifest system" is a paper tracking system that accompanies hazardous substances or waste from the generator to the transporter to the disposal/recycling facility in order to identify who is liable if a problem occurs at any point in the system.

Waste Remediation. The 1986 **Environmental Quality Bond Act (EQBA)** authorized New York State to spend $1.2 billion for investigation and clean-up of inactive hazardous waste sites, $100 million for no-interest loans to help municipalities close nonhazardous solid waste landfills and $250 million for purchase of environmentally sensitive lands (see next section). Monies for these programs are to be raised by the sale of bonds (see Figure 11-4).

131

How a Bond Act Works

A bond act allows the sale of bonds to finance large-scale, long-term projects. Bonds are not usually sold immediately after passage of a bond act. Instead, bond sales occur in stages as expenditures for work on the projects proceed. In this way, interest on the money borrowed is minimized.

To achieve this responsible assumption of debt, the state prefinances bond act program expenditures from an existing fund. This prefinancing works as follows: each year, agencies submit budget requests for specific amounts of money to carry out bond act programs. The legislature appropriates the money to the agencies from the state Capital Projects Fund, and work is carried out. Project bills are paid from this appropriation as each stage of work or acquisition is completed.

After payments have been made for bond act work, the New York State Comptroller sells general obligation bonds, and bond proceeds are used to reimburse the Capital Projects Fund. The comptroller chooses the timing and amount of bond sale and may defer the sale of bonds until bond market conditions are judged to be most favorable to the taxpayers. As a result, bonds may not necessarily be sold in the same year in which bondable expenditures are made.

Figure 11-4

To date 1016 sites throughout the state are known or thought to have received hazardous waste in the past. About 285 of these sites pose a significant environmental threat or human health problems. The Department of Environmental Conservation has developed a New York State Inactive Hazardous Waste Site Remedial Plan which will:

- investigate and rank all potential hazardous waste sites based on their "significant threat to the environment"
- induce responsible parties to undertake and fund clean-up activities wherever possible
- use state funding to remediate sites where responsible parties are unknown, unwilling, or unable to cooperate, and where federal Superfund monies are not available.

Natural Resources Management

Natural resources management promotes and coordinates the state's water, wetlands, forests and lands, fish and wildlife, marine and mineral resources. The Department of Environmental Conservation is mandated to assure their protection, enhancement, allocation and balanced use for the public benefit.

Resources management includes maintenance and improvement of our natural resources including such activities as permitting wetlands utilization, issuing hunting and fishing licenses, stocking programs for reestablishment of species population for sport purposes, permitting use conflict (for example, well-withdrawal permits on Long Island), protecting endangered and threatened species, permitting oil and natural gas mines, protecting against forest fires, and conducting search/resource efforts by the state forest rangers.

FISH AND WILDLIFE

The Division of Fish and Wildlife is organized in five major program areas: environmental protection, environmental management, species management, public use, and extension services. Activities of these programs include: species inventory and monitoring, trout stream stocking, deer population management, and increased public access.

Environmental protection programs maintain productive habitats for fish and wildlife in addition to protecting unique and essential environments. Most recent studies have focused on the impacts of acid deposition (acid rain), small hydroelectric facilities, and toxic contaminants in fish and wildlife.

One of the most popular programs in this division is the rearing and stocking of more than one million pounds per year of trout, salmon and warmwater gamefish in New York's lakes and streams. Optimum access and availability of fishing and other wildlife recreation has had a positive economic impact on the state's economy.

Extension services gain public support for wise management of fish and wildlife resources by making people aware of their value and availability. In 1982, the Return A Gift To Wildlife Program (RGTW) was established to fund a variety of education, conservation, and restoration projects aimed at improving New York's fish and wildlife resources and the public's enjoyment of them. Donations are made through a check-off procedure on the New York State Income Tax forms. Since 1983, over $10 billion has been contributed to the program.

LANDS AND FORESTS

Goals for the Division of Lands and Forests encompass management and protection of state-owned lands; forestry programs including harvesting and marketing of wood products outside the forest preserves and urban education projects; administration of the state pesticide program; and acquisition of lands and easements for DEC programs.

The Department of Environmental Conservation administers more than 3.7 million acres of land, including the Adirondack (2.6 million) and Catskill (280,000) Forest Preserves, and more than 750,000 acres of reforestation and multiple-use areas across the state. Forest rangers within these preserves suppress wildfires, conduct educational programs, direct search and rescue efforts for persons lost or injured, and administer the state's outdoor guide licensing program.

The Adirondack Park Agency (APA) was created in 1971 to develop long range land use plans for both public and private lands within the park. The APA also administers two other state laws within the park: the **Wild, Scenic and Recreation Rivers System Act** (1972) and the **Freshwater Wetlands Act** (1975). Through a land use permit system the APA seeks to control the impact of development on this unique wilderness preserve.

Land acquisition programs have been funded by the **Environmental Quality Bond Acts** of 1972 and 1986. Lands are purchased for a variety of reasons including increased recreational opportunities and access; protection of ecologically sensitive areas; consolidation of existing holdings; and preservation of scenic areas.

Management of pesticides is accomplished through training and certification of private (mainly farmers) and commercial applicators; registration of pesticide businesses; registration of all pesticides sold and used in the state; and enforcement and administration of all pesticide laws and regulations. For example, in 1986 DEC prohibited the use of diazinon on golf courses and sod farms because the Fish and Wildlife Division's pathology unit documented the association of the presence of diazinon with high incidents of bird mortality. This led the U.S. Environmental Protection Agency (EPA) to cancel the registration of diazinon. This was the first such cancellation of a pesticide based on wildlife hazards alone. Other pesticides such as chlordane, aldrin, dieldrin, and heptachlor are targeted to be banned in New York State.

MARINE RESOURCES

The marine resources division manages and monitors the conditions of New York State's marine crustaceans, finfish, shellfish, and seashore habitats. Tidal wetlands are identified for acquisition using EQBA funds with the division managing these lands in cooperation with local governments to ensure appropriate public use and long term preservation.

Biologists monitor marine populations of targeted species and develop procedures to protect and maintain them as a healthy resource. Studies of the American lobster and certain shellfish are evaluating the impacts of commercial harvesting, tidal pollutions, and tidal wetland development on species population levels.

MINERAL RESOURCES

New York State ranks eleventh in the nation in the production of nonfuel minerals and leads the nation in the production of calcium chloride, garnet, and emery. Crushed stone, cement, zinc, sand, and gravel are also mined. Such fossil fuels as oil and natural gas are mined as well.

The Division of Mineral Resources controls the drilling and production of oil, natural gas, and solution salt and regulates other types of mining to assure reclamation of mined land. The regulatory program emphasizes protection of the land, water, and air through environmentally sound drilling practices, proper disposal of drilling fluids, restoration of mine and drilling sites, and proper plugging of exhausted and abandoned wells. A permit/inspection system is used to ensure compliance with the regulations. New York State has the most stringent aquifer drilling requirements in the United States.

Regulations and Enforcement

Two New York State laws are essential to the entire environmental regulatory process: the **State Environmental Quality Review Act** of 1975 (**SEQRA**) and the **Uniform Procedures Act** of 1977. SEQRA was developed to help the government and the public protect and improve the environment by requiring that environmental factors be considered along with social and economic considerations in government decision making. An **environmental impact statement (EIS)** identifies significant or negative effects on the environment for a particular project and examines ways to reduce or avoid these adverse environmental impacts.

The State Environmental Quality Review Act applies to any state or local government agency whenever it must approve or fund a private or public project. Project applicants may be responsible for preparing the environmental impact statement.

The Uniform Procedures Act compliments the SEQRA process by putting into the code of regulations the permit application and review process, from regional staff review to a public hearing conducted by an administrative law judge.

Environmental analysts, located in all nine of DEC's regional offices, review these permit applications. Status of projects and activities subject to DEC regulations are published weekly in the *Environmental Notice Bulletin*.

The Division of Regulatory Affairs is also responsible for establishing criteria for siting and design of low level radioactive waste disposal facilities. Permit applications for temporary storage or permanent disposal of these wastes are also reviewed by this division. (NOTE: the **Low Level Radioactive Waste Management Act** of 1986 mandated that state-owned facilities be operational by 1993.)

Enforcement of the **Environmental Conservation Laws (ECLs)**, rules and regulations is the role of environmental conservation officers and investigators. Their activities range from protection of endangered species to tracking illegal transport, storage, or disposal of hazardous wastes. Environmental enforcement personnel work closely with regional attorneys and the general counsel to coordinate enforcement efforts.

Environment 2000—The Future

Historically, New Yorkers have had a concern for the protection of the state's natural environment. Even before the state constitutional amendment in 1894 established the Adirondack Park as "forever wild," land use and water quality issues were being addressed on a regional basis. At the same time, New Yorkers have abused other resources, for example, hazardous waste of Love Canal, PCBs (polychlorinated biphenyls) in the Hudson River, groundwater contamination on Long Island, and acid rain in the Adirondacks.

The natural environment is not static. Dynamic forces, both natural and man-made, threaten the quality and quantity of these resources. As we enter the next century, the stewardship role of the Department of Environmental Conservation will be to strike a balance between protection of our natural resources and pressures for economic development.

TRANSPORTATION AND INFRASTRUCTURE

History

A state department for transportation was the first agency formed by New York State. At the end of the Revolutionary War, the Office of Surveyor-General was established to survey lands vested in the State of New York. In 1817, the state engineer was charged with digging the Erie Canal which was completed in eight years. By 1946, a combined Office of State Engineer and Surveyor was established and renamed the Department of Public Works.

The "good roads" movement began in New York as the state's privately owned dirt turnpikes became 81,000 miles of paved public highways. The Department of Highways was established as a result of the **Highway Act** of 1909.

Prosperous times followed World War II and resulted in many Americans purchasing automobiles in unprecedented numbers. The ideal of individual mobility was now a reality, as personal travel by automobile more than quadrupled in the state.

This new mobility spurred expansion of commerce and an exodus of people from the cities to the suburbs. More highways were built to accommodate increased traffic travelling at greater speeds. The parkways constructed in the 1920s and 1930s, and the thruway system constructed in the 1950s, became models for the nation's Interstate Highway System which was built during the 1960s and 1970s.

During the 1960s, while the Interstate Highway System was under construction, there was increasing demand for air travel and an expansion of the state's ports. To coordinate the development of each transportation mode, the Department of Transportation (DOT) was formed in 1969. The mandate of the department was to provide adequate, safe, balanced, and efficient transportation at reasonable costs to the people of New York State.

Administration

Under the leadership of the Commissioner of Transportation who is appointed by the governor, the Department of Transportation's central office in Albany coordinates the work of the 11 regional offices throughout the state (see Figure 11-5). Each regional office is headed by a regional director who is responsible for delivering services and completing construction and maintenance programs within that region.

The planning staff reviews all proposed projects to ensure that there is a balance between competing transportation needs. Project plans and specifications are developed by a team of specialists: engineers, lab technicians, draftsmen, landscape architects, cartographers, photogrammatists, and computer analysts.

Project construction is performed by private contractors who bid competitively for each job. DOT engineers monitor and inspect construction projects to ensure work is completed to contract specifications. Another important concern is that traffic through the construction zone is adequately protected. Safety of travelers and workers are a prime concern.

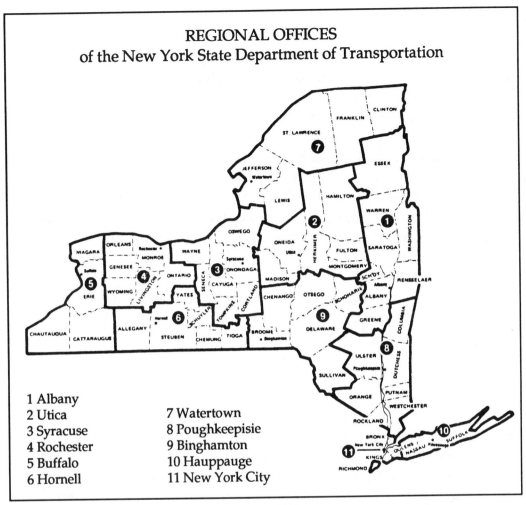

REGIONAL OFFICES
of the New York State Department of Transportation

1 Albany
2 Utica
3 Syracuse
4 Rochester
5 Buffalo
6 Hornell

7 Watertown
8 Poughkeepisie
9 Binghamton
10 Hauppauge
11 New York City

Figure 11-5

Highways and Streets

The Division of Highway Maintenance is the largest in the DOT and is responsible for the safe operation of the state's 15,000 miles of highways and some 7000 bridges. Providing assistance to local governments, the DOT helps operate and maintain an additional 95,000 miles of local roads and nearly 11,000 bridges. Activities of this division include: pavement repair and marking, snow and ice control, bridge repair, sign upkeep, shoulder and guard-rail repair, roadside mowing, litter removal, and rest-area maintenance.

Public Transportation

Each year, there are over 2 billion bus, ferry, and subway commuter passengers in New York State. Public authorities, local governments, private corporations, and nonprofit human services agencies own and operate public transit facilities in the state.

The Department of Transportation's program for capital assistance provides for purchasing buses and constructing new terminals and garages. In addition, DOT is responsible for regulating the safety, service, and fare aspects of private intrastate bus operations. DOT conducts safety inspections of privately-owned vehicles providing public services and school buses.

The Public Transportation Safety Board investigates public transit accidents involving commuter rail, subways, buses, and their physical facilities.

Railroads

New York's rail freight network consists of two major east-west mainlines and connecting branchlines and shortlines. Partnership between the state, private industries, rail owners and local governments has revitalized the railroads. Improvements by Amtrak and the DOT have produced a growing passenger rail system connecting 26 communities across the state as well as many major northeastern and midwestern cities and cities in Canada including Toronto and Montréal.

Railroads are monitored for compliance with federal and state safety regulations. Rail accidents and citizen complaints are investigated by DOT.

Aviation

Every few seconds, an airplane takes off or lands somewhere in the state. Over half of these air passengers travel for business purposes.

The Department of Transportation provides financial aid and technical assistance to over 480 public and private airports. The department helps in planning for future aviation projects and provides funds for capital improvements.

The Department of Transportation also owns and operates Steward International Airport and the Republic Airport.

Waterways and Ports

New York State's major waterways—the Hudson River, Great Lakes, the St. Lawrence Seaway, and the New York State Canal System—provide a water link throughout the state.

The Department of Transportation owns and operates 524 miles of canals, consisting of the Erie, Champlain, Oswego, and Cayuga/Seneca Canals. Each year, approximately 150,000 recreational boats travel through the 57 locks along with important commercial traffic. The canals are also a source of hydropower, flood control, fresh water supply, and farm irrigation.

The ports of New York City, Albany, Buffalo, Oswego, and Ogdensburg play a vital economic role in both national and international trade. DOT provides planning, technical assistance, and state loans and grants to port authorities for equipment or facility construction and rehabilitation.

Financing Improvements

In the 1960s and early 1970s, highway expansion was the emphasis but little attention was given to the upkeep of existing roads. The financial recession of the mid-1970s forced New York State to cut back on many state programs, including road and highway maintenance. The 1973 oil crisis resulted in many drivers purchasing energy efficient cars. Tax revenues to state and local governments were further reduced. Although the transportation infrastructure was subject to more wear and tear, fewer fuel tax revenues were available for the necessary repairs. Inflation also decreased construction buying power. State and local governments were forced to reduce their budgets and workforces for maintenance and repair.

The resulting **infrastructure neglect** affected all modes of transportation. New York State experienced collapsing bridges, congested highways, bankrupt railroads. Disrepair plagued ports, canals, airports, and commuter rail lines.

In 1983, New York State voters approved the 1983 **Rebuild New York Transportation Infrastructure Renewal Bond Act**. The $1.25 billion Bond Act targeted infrastructure rehabilitation. (Total federal/state funds totaled seven billion dollars.) Nicknamed the "Rebuilding New York" Initiative, it called for:

- the rebuilding and repairing of state highways, parkways and bridges
- the improvement of local highways and bridges
- elimination of highway - railroad grade crossings
- construction of commuter rail parking facilities
- construction and repair of rail rapid transit, commuter rail, rail passenger and freight facilities, airport and aviation capital projects
- repairing and improving ports, marine terminals, canals and waterways.

A second Bond Act, called the **Accelerated Capacity and Transportation Improvements of the Nineties Bond Act** was passed by the voters in 1988. It authorized $3 billion to assure continued construction, reconstruction, capacity improvement, replacement, reconditioning and preservation of the state's highways and bridges. Expenditures are divided by region with New York City and Long Island receiving 23 percent; the Hudson Valley 40 percent; and the rest of the state 40 percent. The Bond Act consists of three programs: highways, capacity improvements, and state and municipal bridges. Through a memorandum of understanding, the state legislature determines the priority of the projects that are undertaken

PART IV

STATE POLITICS

The U.S. Constitution makes no mention of political parties, but they have become essential instruments of representative government, serving as intermediaries between groups of citizens and governmental institutions. Through them, registered party members band together to advocate their collective preferences for policy choices. Organized on local, state, and national levels, parties provide the mechanism for the nomination of candidates and the management of their campaigns. In addition, parties play a significant role in staffing the executive branch of government and in building majorities for decision-making by the legislative branch.

CHAPTER 12
POLITICAL PARTIES

The party system is undergoing an unprecedented decline both in New York State and in the nation, in spite of its significant functions. In some ways this decline is changing the traditional American method of keeping government responsive to the electorate. Public distaste for party politics is evident everywhere. Although it is much easier to register and vote today than it was 15 years ago, the percentage of citizens who do so is steadily decreasing. Both major parties have lost members to voters who consider themselves as independents, that is, those who choose not to belong to any party. And those who do belong often do not identify strongly with their party.

The reasons are not hard to identify. Ethical abuses by governmental employees have subverted the political process, from the presidential level on down, which has turned many away from the parties. Media and public relations advisors able to package a candidate as a marketable item, have replaced the party as the originator of campaign strategy. Poll takers, rather than the party platform, are likely to be the source of a candidate's positions. The mass media are replacing parties in their role of informing the electorate about the candidates. Finally, personality politics and media-centered campaigns siphon workers and contributors away from the party.

Many who use the political processes today are impatient with the loose consensus politics that has traditionally held together each of the two major parties. Political activists who focus their energy on single issue organizations tend to weaken the major parties by depriving them of members with important political know-how and financial support.

Surprisingly perhaps, the one man, one vote principle, which has improved the equality of our representation in federal, state and local legislative bodies, has also done its share to undermine party organization. Districts, created solely on the basis of population, and structured along town, city and county lines, tend to produce candidates with few ties to party organizations.

In this changing world, minor parties have gained in influence. In some instances, their candidates attract enough votes to prevent the major party nominees from achieving a plurality. By cross-endorsing a major party nominee, minor parties may gain positions of influence greater than their membership warrants.

Another blow to the two-party system has been its growing inability to command patronage. At one time, the party that prevailed in an election was represented in government not only by the candidates it placed in office, but by the people it recommended for appointment to government posts, both small and large. At its best, the patronage system provided people to carry out the policies of the party the voters had elected, and provided rewards and incentives for those who had supported the party and volunteered their efforts. At its worst, it substituted party loyalty for competence as a qualification for a government job. In either case, it was the strength of the party. Today, much of the government bureaucracy is ruled by civil service qualifications rather than the patronage system; thus, the parties have fewer rewards to offer those who serve them.

In recent years, campaign finance laws (see Chapter 13) have subjected parties to strict accounting and disclosure regulations. Changes in party rules assure all factions a stronger role in decision making, from local and state primaries to presidential nominating conventions. Paradoxically, with all their problems, or because of them, parties today are more accessible than ever before to the influence of voters who wish to use the political vehicle they provide.

WHAT IS A PARTY?

A recognized political party, according to the **New York State Election Law,** is one whose candidate for governor won at least 50,000 votes in the previous gubernatorial election. There are now five recognized parties in New York State: Democratic, Republican, Conservative, Right to Life and Liberal. The order in which they are listed on the ballot is determined by the number of votes each received in the previous gubernatorial election. A recognized party is expected to maintain a year-round organization and participate in primaries. Other political groups, which the election Law calls "independent bodies," may organize to run one or more candidates in a single election.

PARTY ENROLLMENT

Enrolled party members are entitled to vote in that party's primary elections, sign nominating petitions, hold party office and participate in party caucuses.

During central or local registration, or when registering by mail, voters may enroll in the party of their choice, may choose not to enroll in any party, or may change their enrollment. Change of enrollment goes into effect only after the following general election, although exceptions are made for those newly turned 18, newly naturalized, or newly resident in the state, and, in some cases, for those who have moved.

HOW ARE PARTIES ORGANIZED?

General rules for the organization of political parties are established in the **New York State Election Law**. For example, the Law provides for party organization and outlines the manner in which party positions may be filled and how parties and independent groups may nominate candidates for public office. Within these legal guidelines, however, there is some flexibility for parties to establish their own rules. Therefore, structure varies from one party to another and, to some extent, from one county to another.

The Election District

The building blocks of party organization are the election districts, sometimes referred to as precincts or wards, each consisting of no more than 950 registered voters. These election districts are the smallest political units in the state; they are the scene of the proverbial grass roots party activity where the party faithful work to win votes for the party's candidates and to get voters to the polls. Except in the cities of New York, and Buffalo, and in the counties of Monroe, Nassau and Suffolk where election districts are drawn by the boards of elections, these units are established by town boards and city councils. The small size of these election districts gives parties great flexibility to organize as political units within any district from which candidates are elected to public office, such as congressional, State Assembly or Senate districts.

Enrolled party members within each election district choose two committee members, usually one man and one woman (except where party rules permit the election of three or four from each district). Committee members must be residents of the Assembly district in which their election districts are located.

The Local Party Committee

All the committee members in each unit of government together choose the local (city, town or village) party chairperson and other officers. This committee is then responsible for party activity in the community—obtaining signatures for petitions, registering voters, getting out the vote, raising money, and conducting local campaigns. For purely local offices in cities or towns, the chairperson and executive members of the city or town committee usually select the candidate who is then endorsed by the whole committee. Candidates for town and village offices are in some cases chosen at party caucuses open to all party members.

Local party organizations may be aided by local political clubs which are semisocial, semipolitical centers for party members. Although it has no official party status or role, a club in many places serves as the local campaign headquarters and as a meeting place for both party leaders and for rank-and-file members. It is the place to which the party member traditionally has come to seek advice on ways to obtain help or information from public officials.

The County Committee—Base of Party Power

The committee members in all the election districts in the county make up the county committee which, in turn, elects county party officers. The county party organization is the basic unit of party machinery. Within limits, these county organizations may make party rules to govern their operations. There may be a good deal of variation between parties, and within parties from one county to another.

Candidates for the House of Representatives, state legislature, and county-wide offices (including county-level judgeships) are generally designated by the county committee acting as a whole or by the county executive committee, according to party rules in a particular county.

Except in New York City (the state's only city that contains more than one county) each county organization has an executive committee made up of city, ward, and town chairpersons, plus other elected officers.

Party Organization in New York City

In New York City, there is no formal citywide political organization but each of its five counties has an executive committee composed of assembly district leaders and other officers. These district leaders are elected directly by the enrolled voters. This executive committee, or in some cases, the whole county committee, elects the county chairperson.

The Assembly district leaders and committees handle nominations for assemblymen and wield considerable influence over the choice of candidates for state senator, United States representatives and for major city offices. As in other parts of the state, the county party organization, through its leader, exercises political power through patronage and through the influence it exerts on elected officials.

The State Committee

State committee members are elected for two-year terms from such districts as the rules of the party may provide. The county leaders have a major voice in selecting the persons who will run for state committee positions in each district within the county.

The state committee elects a state chairperson and an executive committee, it adopts a party platform, raises money for the party, designates the party's candidates for statewide offices, chooses the chairperson and delegates-at-large for national party nominating conventions at which the party's presidential candidates are named, and selects the party's slate of presidential electors. The state committee also chooses the man and woman to serve on the national committee.

Party committees at all levels are elected. Party officers, who are the most visible party functionaries, are then named by the committees.

HOW THE PARTY CHOOSES ITS CANDIDATES
FOR PUBLIC OFFICE

Party organizations have the initial role in nominating persons for public as well as for party office. Normally the party leadership at the appropriate level indicates its preferred choices and causes designating petitions to be circulated on behalf of its candidates. When there is no challenge to the leadership choice, the filing of that candidate's petitions constitutes election to party office, or nomination to public office.

If there is any opposition within the party to this choice, challengers may circulate their own petitions and the outcome is settled at a primary election. The election law specifies the dates for circulating and filing the petitions and the numbers of signatures required for candidates in each size district (for example, fewer signatures would be required for petitions in an Assembly than in a congressional district).

Primary elections and the circulation of petitions have these aspects in common: only voters enrolled in the party may vote in its primary, and only enrolled party members may circulate or sign petitions for a party candidate.

A special provision that applies only to New York City, requires contestants for nomination to citywide office to capture at least 40 percent of the party vote in the primary. If no candidate does so, the nomination will be decided in a runoff primary between the two front-runners.

Although regulations surrounding primary contests are detailed and complex, the system does permit any group or individual to appeal to the members of the party when it disagrees with the actions of the leadership.

Nomination To Statewide Office

Since 1968, New York State has had a challenge primary system for selecting party candidates for statewide public office. Candidates may be designated by a majority vote of the state party committee. Any candidate who receives 25 percent of the vote in the state committee, however, is entitled to seek the party designation in a statewide primary.

Even candidates who fail to win this percentage may force a statewide primary by gathering 20,000 signatures with at least 100 in each of half the state's congressional districts. This alternative clearly adds to the expenses of the challenger. The relative ease this system affords to candidates to appeal directly to the party voters has encouraged a growing number of candidates to vie for the support of the overall party membership. The challenge primary system in New York has thus reinforced a tendency for political aspirants to act independently of the established party organization. The number of candidate-centered organizations these separate party contestants put together also tends to draw and divert strength from party organizations.

INDEPENDENT NOMINATIONS

A person does not have to belong to or have the backing of a recognized party to run for office. The election law spells out the way that independent bodies may organize to nominate candidates by circulating petitions to put their names on the ballot. Because independent candidates are not involved in primaries, a much larger number of signatures is required for their petitions than for regular party designating petitions. Independent petitions are circulated during specified periods after the party petition period, and a candidate who has failed to win the party designation may subsequently file to run as an independent. In addition, voters can write-in (and vote for) candidates not listed on the ballot.

CHAPTER 13
ELECTIONS—THE VOTERS AND THE CANDIDATES

Americans describe their system of government as a democracy; a system equally committed to majority rule and to the protection of individual and minority rights, or, in the words of Abraham Lincoln, *"government of the people, by the people, and for the people."* But there can be neither majority rule nor government by the people without elections, and to be meaningful, most citizens must participate in these elections.

THE VOTERS

The U.S. Constitution provides that no state may deny the vote to those 18 years old or older. The federal **Voting Rights Act** of 1965 and its subsequent amendments prohibit all tests of literacy; and the Supreme Court has held invalid all state qualifications on the length of time an eligible citizen must be a resident in order to vote. A state may, however, permit registration lists to close a reasonable time before an election, and New York State does so 30 days before the day of the general election. Even this restriction cannot bar a person from voting in presidential elections, and special federal ballots are available to those who move after the closing of the registration lists.

Although some obstacles remain; for example, the prior registration requirement and the refusal of some communities to allow their college students to vote locally, the franchise has effectively been guaranteed to all citizens. However, voter apathy has made voter turnout in the United States among the lowest of the world's major democracies. We say that Ronald Reagan was elected by a landslide in 1984 because he won approximately 60 percent of the vote, but since only 53 percent of the eligible population voted, Mr. Reagan was actually elected by 31 percent. Looking at it in another way, seven out of ten people either voted for someone else or did not vote at all.

Who Can Vote?

A person is qualified to vote in New York State if he/she is:

- A United States citizen
- 18 years old or older on or before Election Day
- A resident of New York State and of his or her county, city or village for 30 days by Election Day
- Registered to vote in the election district of residence.

Who Cannot Vote?

- Convicted felons, until they have served their sentences or have completed parole
- Those who have been committed to a mental institution by court order or have been judged legally incompetent
- People who are on probation and those in prison who are awaiting trial or serving time for misdemeanors may vote.

Administration Of Elections

In 1974, the New York State Legislature established a New York State Board of Elections, for the first time centralizing responsibility for administering elections in the state. The change largely eliminated diverse interpretations of the law that had produced different registration and voting procedures from county to county.

Local boards of election in each of the 57 counties and in the City of New York continue the day to day supervision of registration and voting, but are guided by the state board which issues advice and direction on the detailed and constantly changing New York State Election Law.

In addition, the state board has specific power:

- to issue instructions and promulgate rules and regulations for "the administration of the election process" as well as of campaign practices
- to visit, inspect and, if necessary, investigate practices in the county and New York City boards of elections

- to prepare uniform forms for use by local election officials in the conduct of registration and voting
- to report annually to the governor on the effectiveness of the election laws and to make any necessary recommendations for reform
- and to take "all appropriate steps" to encourage the broadest possible voter participation in elections.

To enforce its authority, the board has subpoena power; can bring judicial proceedings in the state Supreme Court; and refer any of its findings and complaints to the district attorney in the county where any violation of the law or of the board's rules takes place.

The New York State Board of Elections is an agency of the Executive Department. However, military voting continues to be administered through the Department of State.

The board of elections consists of four salaried members appointed by the governor for two-year, staggered terms. The governor must select each commissioner from a separate list—one each submitted by the state Republican and the state Democratic Party Chairman; one submitted by the Democratic leaders of the Senate and the Assembly acting jointly; and one by the Republican leaders of the two houses.

Local boards of elections are generally made up of two commissioners, one selected by each of the two major party chairpersons and subsequently appointed by the county legislative body. New York City has ten who are appointed by the city council, one Republican and one Democrat from each of the city's five boroughs.

In the conduct of registration and voting, these boards appoint all election employees on a bipartisan basis, giving the two major parties an equal and exclusive representation in all electoral activity. This bipartisan system is designed to safeguard the electoral process and deter fraud, but critics contend that it shuts out other recognized parties and independents from election administration. Some advocate bringing the conduct of elections under the civil service umbrella and eliminating the party role in administration.

The basic unit of election administration within each county and borough is the election district. There are nearly 15,000 such districts in the state. Most are established by town boards or city councils under election law standards that provide for up to 950 registered voters per district. In New York City, Buffalo, and in the counties of Nassau, Suffolk, and Monroe, election districts are established by the boards of elections.

Each district has four election inspectors, two from each party. This board of inspectors is in charge of local registration and election day activity and its members are compensated on an hourly or per diem basis for their service.

Registration Procedures

New York has a statewide system of **permanent personal registration** (PPR). This enables a voter, after initially registering, to remain permanently registered to vote unless he or she moves or fails to vote in a general election, primary, or special election within a four year period. In that case, the voter will be notified by the local board of elections and must respond to the notice by reinstating his or her registration, or it will be cancelled.

In 1975, the legislature adopted a system of registration by mail. Voters may obtain mail registration forms from their boards of elections, town and city clerks, political parties, public libraries, post offices or The League of Women Voters. The completed forms must be received at the county board of elections within 25 days of the general election if the voter is to participate in that election.

Voters may register in person during normal business hours at the central board of elections from December 1 to the end of August, on a date announced each year. Voters may also register in person during a local registration day in late September or early October. City, town or village clerks are responsible for designating and announcing places for local registration, but generally these are the local polling places.

Counties with 300,000 or more population must have two days of local registration a year, one of which must be on a Saturday. Smaller counties may have one local registration day a year (which must be on a Saturday) except in the year of a presidential election when two days are required.

The availability of mail registration has made absentee registration procedures unnecessary. However, the election law makes special provision for absentee registration for resident patients at veterans hospitals. Members of the armed services and their families register and vote under special procedures administered by the Division of Servicemen's Voting.

In New York State, a voter may choose to enroll in one of the five recognized parties: Democratic, Republican, Conservative, Right to Life, and Liberal. A voter may decline to enroll in any party. Party enrollment and registration lists are available for public inspection at the county boards of elections. Only enrolled members of a party can vote in that party's primary elections. On Election Day, registered voters may vote as they please.

Types Of Elections In New York State

The political calendar, set each year by the legislature, is built around the date of the primary. It specifies dates for party caucuses, gathering and filing petitions, and sets other deadlines for candidates and party purposes. A copy of this calendar is available at each county board of elections, or it may be obtained from the state board of elections.

A general election is held every year on the first Tuesday after the first Monday in November. Presidential elections are held every fourth year. In even-numbered years, elections are held for U.S. Representatives, one third of the members of the U.S. Senate, state legislators, and some county officials; and every fourth year for Governor, Lieutenant-Governor, Comptroller, and Attorney General. Most local and city officials are elected in odd-numbered years. Judges may be elected at any election depending on the expiration of their terms. State and local ballot issues may also appear on the ballots at any election.

Primaries are party elections. They are held in New York State only when there is a contest within a party for nomination as a candidate to a public office or for election to a party office. Where there is no contest, there is no primary. The election law provides for a runoff primary in New York City in the event that candidates for major city offices do not receive at least 40 percent of the vote. Again, only enrolled party members are entitled to vote in the runoff.

Because the timing of the primary has important political implications, the legislature frequently changes its date by amending the Election Law. A late primary is thought to benefit incumbents. Early primaries are preferred by challengers who need time to become known. The primary date is now set in September. In presidential election years, an additional primary is held in the spring for the election of delegates to the national nominating conventions which take place in mid-summer.

Village elections are usually held either on the third Tuesday in March or the third Tuesday in June. Village residents who are registered with their county board of elections qualify whether or not the village has personal registration. A day of registration is available to those not otherwise registered.

When someone in office dies or resigns, a special election may be held to fill the vacancy. In those cases, the governor sets the date for the special election.

School elections and annual meetings are held in May or June and are governed by the Education Law rather than the Election Law. In central and union free school districts, the school budget must also be submitted to the voters. Members of all boards of education are elected except in the cities of New York and Yonkers where they are appointed, although within New York City, members of community boards are elected (see Chapter 9).

Some school districts do not require voter registration; others have special registration for their own elections and use voter registration lists from the board of elections. The same voting requirements pertain to school elections as to general elections, with one exception. In New York City parents of a school child do not have to be citizens to qualify as voters in a community school board election and may register for such elections either in the district where their child attends school or in the district where they live.

Election Day Procedures

Polls are open from 6 A.M.-9 P.M. across the state for the general election and from 12 noon until 9 P.M. at the primaries except in New York City and Nassau, Suffolk, Erie, Westchester, Rockland, Orange and Ulster Counties where polls are open from 6 A.M. until 9 P.M. Electioneering is prohibited within a distance of 100 feet from each polling place. The local board of inspectors is responsible for maintaining order and for carrying out the provisions of the Election Law.

Voting machines are mandatory in all general elections, in primary elections in New York City, and in all contested primaries outside New York City where there are 950 or more enrolled eligible voters. If an election district has more than 800 voters, an additional voting machine may be used.

Inspectors must give instructions on the use of the voting machine to those voters who request it and each precinct is required to have a sample ballot. Voters who require assistance in operating the voting machine because of a physical handicap or illiteracy may receive help from anyone of their choice. It is a felony to vote illegally or to assist another person to do so.

Voters who are refused the right to vote at the polls have two courses of action:
• Voters may request and sign an affidavit that they are registered to vote in that election district. They then can vote by paper ballot; each ballot will be returned to the board of elections and counted only if board records uphold the voters' affidavit. If ballots are not counted, the board notifies voters that they are not registered, and sends them a mail-registration form.
• Voters may appeal at once to a Supreme Court justice or to a judge of the County Court for court orders requiring that they be permitted to vote. These courts must stay in session during election hours to receive such appeals, which take precedence over other litigation. With a court order, the voters vote on the voting machine.

Candidates have a specified period after the vote has been tallied to challenge the count. The Supreme Court may order machines impounded and a recount undertaken. Final results are officially announced by the state board of elections.

Absentee Voting

Voters may request absentee ballots for general elections, village elections, primaries, and for special elections called by the governor. Some school districts permit absentee voting for school board elections, but not for school budgets or other ballot issues, nor for special school district elections.

Registered voters who are ill, physically disabled, or away from their county of residence or from New York City on Election Day are eligible for absentee ballots. Absentee ballot applications are available from the county boards of election at any time between the opening of central registration, usually about December 1, and the Monday preceding the election. Voters may also apply during local registration days.

Applications mailed to the board of elections must be received there at least seven days before the election; voters who apply in person may do so up to 24 hours before the election. All completed absentee ballots must be postmarked no later than the day before the election or delivered to the polling place before the polls close on Election Day.

THE CANDIDATES

Despite numerous complaints about the length, quality, cost, and many other aspects of political campaigns, the only legal restrictions placed upon candidates for political office are in the area of campaign finance.

Financing Campaigns

In recent years, television, polling, sampling, direct mail and other modern campaign techniques that candidates use to reach enormous numbers of people have all helped to escalate the cost of running for office. To prevent potential candidates from relying too heavily on large donors seeking influence, the state board of elections was established to supervise campaign financing as well as to administer registration and voting. Soon after the law was framed, courts struck down limits on spending as an unconstitutional barrier to freedom of speech. However, limits on contributions are still in force.

The maximum that a single contributor may make to a candidate running for statewide office (Governor, Lieutenant-Governor, Comptroller and Attorney General) is an amount equal to one-half cent per enrolled voter in the primary, and one-half cent per registered voter in the general election. The limit on the amount that members of a candidate's family can give collectively is two and a half cents per registered voter.

In primary, special, or general elections for other than statewide office, a single donor may contribute up to five cents a voter or $50,000, whichever is less, except that the candidate's family may give up to $100,000. The U.S. Supreme Court has ruled that no limit may be put on the amount that a candidate and spouse can contribute to the campaign.

The total that any one donor may contribute in a single year to all political campaigns is set at $150,000; corporations are permitted to contribute $5,000 to all campaigns.

Campaign financing reform, including public funding, continues to remain an area of concern and controversy at both the state and local level. Political action committees, known as PACs, multiplied and gained in influence after the 1974 legislation on campaign finance. Although their activities and finances are strictly regulated under the law, they provide a mechanism whereby any group, including business corporations and labor unions may channel funds to a candidate's election campaign or to a campaign on a ballot issue.

The law sets other limits on campaign practices, including:

- stringent reporting requirements on all campaign receipts and expenditures
- provisions to identify all contributors
- prohibitions against accepting any contribution of more than $100 except by check or other signed draft.

Fair Campaign Practices

At present, New York State has no law to protect against unfair campaign practices. A **Fair Campaign Code** was adopted in 1975 but it was declared unconstitutional by the United States Supreme Court because it did not provide for judicial review of administrative decisions made by the New York State Board of Elections. Since then, legislation for a new code that would meet constitutional guidelines has been introduced repeatedly but the legislature has yet to adopt it.

Some of the practices that a Fair Campaign Code would prohibit are: deliberate misrepresentation of a candidate's viewpoints or actions; misuse of the results of opinion polls; fraudulent or untrue endorsements of a candidate; doctored photographs or writings of a candidate; political espionage.

Judicial Campaigns

In order to preserve public confidence in the impartial administration of justice, candidates for judicial office are generally prohibited from engaging in political activity. Since most New York State judges must run for office in partisan elections, however, this general prohibition is modified for a specific period of time before and after the election to allow judicial candidates to participate to a limited degree in their own campaigns. In general, judges and their personal appointees are prohibited from participating, either directly or indirectly, in any political campaign for any office, except their own campaigns. Furthermore, judges may not be officers in political parties and may not make political contributions.

A candidate's committee may solicit funds, but campaign rhetoric must be limited. For instance, candidates cannot discuss controversial legal or political issues which might come before the court such as abortion. They are restricted to talking about their own qualifications and those of their opponents, or about measures to improve the law, the legal system or the administration of justice.

The political activity of candidates for judicial office is governed by the **Rules Governing Judicial Conduct**, by the **Code of Judicial Conduct** and by the New York State Election Law. The New York State Commission on Judicial Conduct has the responsibility of enforcement.

PART V
ACCESS TO GOVERNMENT

Across the country in the early 1970's, public concern over the conduct of public officials generated new interest in open government. This concern gave rise to a number of "sunshine" laws and policies governing access to information, open meetings and regulations of lobbyists. More recently, considerable concern has been expressed in relation to establishing ethical standards for government officials.

In New York State, the **Freedom of Information Law** went into effect in 1974. Three years later the Open Meetings Law took effect and the Committee on Public Access to Records was established to oversee the implementation of both laws. Later, in 1983, the committee's name was changed to Committee on Open Government. This committee operates under the New York State Department of State and is composed of 11 members, five from government and six from the public. The five government members are: the lieutenant-governor; the secretary of state; the commissioner of general services; the director of the budget; and one elected local government official appointed by the governor. The public members are appointed by the governor and the leaders of the Senate and the Assembly. Two of the public members must be or have been representatives of the news media.

The Committee on Open Government, which operates under the New York State Department of State, furnishes advice to government agencies, the public and the news media; issues regulations and advisory opinions; reviews the operation of the law; and reports its observations and recommendations annually to the governor and the legislature.

Those needing advice regarding either the Freedom of Information Law or the Open Meetings Law should contact: Committee on Open Government, New York State Department of State, 162 Washington Avenue, Albany, NY 12231.

CHAPTER 14
ACCESS TO GOVERNMENT

FREEDOM OF INFORMATION LAW

The Freedom of Information Law assures public access to government records. With certain exceptions, state and local agencies must make their records available to the public and the law also requires that any paper filed or used in local government may be inspected and copied by the public. The law defines the term "agency" to include all units of state and local government, including state agencies, public corporations and authorities as well as any other governmental entity performing a governmental function for the state or a unit of local government. However, the term "agency" does not include the state legislature or the courts. Exempted from public scrutiny are matters of a confidential nature such as medical histories, credit records and personal references.

In some cases, people seeking information from government agencies are refused the information they request. If they feel that the agency is wrong to refuse the information, they may sue the agency and let the court decide whether or not the information should be made available. At one time, many people were unable to take advantage of the intent of the law because they could not afford the cost of going to court. For that reason, the law was amended in 1982 to permit the court to award reasonable attorney's fees and other court costs to plaintiffs able to prove that the information should have been provided. The agency must then pay these costs.

OPEN MEETINGS LAW

The purpose of the **Open Meetings Law** is to assure that government business is conducted openly. The law gives the public the right to attend meetings of public bodies, listen to the discussions and watch the decision making process in action. The law does not, however, guarantee members of the public the right to speak at these meetings.

In the original version of the law, the definition of the term "meetings" was vague. Later, court interpretations of the law defined "meetings" to mean "the official convening of a public body for the purpose of conducting public business." The law applies to all public bodies and "public bodies" is defined to cover entities consisting of two or more people that conduct public business and perform a governmental function for the state, for an agency of the state, or for public corporations such as city councils, town boards, village boards, school boards, zoning boards, commissions, legislative bodies and committees and subcommittees of all those groups.

The law provides for closed or "executive" sessions under certain circumstances. Executive sessions are not separate from open meetings but are a portion of an open meeting from which the public may be excluded. To close a meeting for executive session, a public body must take several steps. First, a motion must be made during an open meeting to enter into executive session. Second, the motion must identify the general area or areas of the subject or subjects to be considered in executive session. Third, the motion must be carried by a majority vote of the total membership of a public body.

It is important to know, however, that a public body cannot close its doors to the public to discuss any subject it chooses since the law also limits the subject matter that may be discussed in executive session. Only certain subjects may be considered in privacy. These include matters of public safety; criminal investigation; current or pending litigation; collective negotiations pertaining to Article 14 of the **Civil Service Law** (the **Taylor Law**); land acquisition; and personal privacy.

The law also requires that notice of the time and place of all meetings be made public in advance of the meeting. Also, minutes of all meetings must be made available. Minutes of open meetings must include a record of all matters formally voted upon and also must include how each member of the body voted. Minutes of executive sessions are required only if action was taken during the session.

The Open Meetings Law does not apply to judicial proceedings, political party committees and caucuses or matters made confidential by federal or state law.

The exemption of political party committees and caucuses from the Open Meetings Law is a cause of concern for proponents of open government. The original law was vague on what matters could be discussed privately in meetings of government officials who are members of the same party. Over time, the courts decided that the intent of the law was to allow only discussions of party business and to prohibit discussion of any subject pertaining to public business. In 1985, the state legislature amended the law to permit party caucuses to discuss any matters they chose, including public business, with the result that matters of public concern can be decided in private by the majority party with only the vote taken in open meetings. This amendment makes it possible for a government body to effectively eliminate public observance of its decision-making process.

LOBBYING REGULATIONS

Lobbyists are persons who seek to influence legislators in regard to proposed laws. They cannot be members of either house. They may represent a specific business or labor group, citizen organization or particular political ideology. In many ways lobbyists can perform a useful function by supplying legislators with information and technical advice on bills and alerting them to the interests of certain groups. However, legislators can be vulnerable to representatives of special interests who can commit large sums of money to further their legislative objectives. The purpose of lobbying regulations is to give the public access to information about such efforts. The law requires any lobbyist or organization that plans to spend more than $2000 toward influencing legislation to register annually and file quarterly itemized reports of expenditures. A Temporary State Commission on Regulation of Lobbying oversees the reporting procedure.

ETHICS

A new ethics code for state officials and employees was passed in 1987. It covers statewide elected officials, state officers and employees, and legislators and legislative employees. For certain purposes, it also covers certain political party chairmen. The law also requires local governments with populations of more than 50,000 to have their own codes of ethics in place by 1991. The **Ethics Law** contains a multitude of provisions. Among other things, it requires financial disclosure by the people it covers. Additionally, it prohibits them from making appearances or providing legal services for private clients in almost all cases involving state agencies and it also prohibits them from selling goods or services to state agencies for amounts greater than $25. A "revolving door" provision covers former state officers and employees and bars them from rendering services on behalf of private clients before their former state agencies for a period of two years from the time of leaving government service. However, there is no bar on former legislators on lobbying, providing they are not paid as lobbyists. Although the law is specific on a large number of things, many people feel that it still contains "ominous gaps and loopholes." To overcome these perceived weaknesses, many amendments to the law continue to be proposed.

APPENDIX:

NEW YORK STATE EXECUTIVE, JUDICIAL, AND ADMINISTRATIVE DEPARTMENTS AND OFFICES

EXECUTIVE:

Governor
Executive Chamber
State Capitol
Albany, NY 12224
518-474-8390

Lieutenant-Governor
State Capitol
Room 326
Albany, NY 12224
518-474-4623

Comptroller
State Office Building
Albany, NY 12236
518-474-4044

Attorney General
State Capitol
Albany, NY 12224
518-474-7124

Board of Elections
P.O. Box 4
1 Commerce Plaza
Albany, NY 12260
518-474-6220

Commission on Domestic Violence
Empire State Plaza
Corning Tower, 28th Floor
Albany, NY 12223
518-473-3655
Crisis Intervention:
1-800-942-6906
Bilingual (Monday-Friday, 9-5):
1-800-942-6908

Commission on Judicial Conduct
Empire State Plaza
(Agency Building 1)
Albany, NY 12223
518-474-5617

Consumer Protection Board
99 Washington Avenue
Albany, NY 12210
518-474-8583

Council for Families and Children
Empire State Plaza
Corning Tower, 28th Floor
Albany, NY 12223
518-474-8038

Council on the Arts
915 Broadway, 7th Floor
New York, NY 10010
212-614-2900

Crime Victims Compensation Board
97 Central Avenue
Albany, NY 12206
518-473-9649

Division for Women
2 World Trade Center
Executive Chamber, 57th Floor
New York, NY 10047
212-587-4408;
State Capitol Executive Chamber
Albany, NY 12224
518-474-3612

Division for Youth
84 Holland Avenue
Albany, NY 12208
518-473-7793

Division of Alcoholism and Alcohol Abuse
194 Washington Avenue
Albany, NY 12210
518-474-3377

Division of the Budget
State Capitol
Albany, NY 12224
518-474-2331

Division of Criminal Justice Services
Executive Park Tower
Albany, NY 12203
518-457-6113

Division of Housing and Community Renewal
1 Fordham Plaza
Bronx, NY 10458;
Empire State Plaza
Corning Tower, Suite 2282
Albany, NY 12220
518-474-8580

Division of Human Rights
55 West 125th Street-
    The Rev. Dr. Martin Luther
    King, Jr. Boulevard
New York, NY 10027
212-870-8400;
Alfred E. Smith Office Building
P.O. Box 7063
Albany, NY 12225-0065
518-474-2705

Division of Substance Abuse
Executive Park South
Albany, NY 12203
518-457-4176;
1-800-522-5353

Energy Office
Empire State Plaza
    (Agency Building 2)
Albany, NY 12223
518-473-4375;
1-800-342-3722

Office for the Aging
Empire State Plaza
    (Agency Building 2)
Albany, NY 12223
518-474-8675;
1-800-342-9871

Office of Employee Relations
Empire State Plaza
    (Agency Building 2)
Albany, NY 12223
518-474-4094

Office of Mental Health
44 Holland Avenue
Albany, NY 12229
518-474-6540

Office of Mental Retardation and Developmental Disabilities
44 Holland Avenue
Albany, NY 12229
518-473-9689

Office of Parks and Recreation And Historic Preservation
Empire State Plaza
    (Agency Building 1)
Albany, NY 12238
518-474-0456

JUDICIAL:

Office of Court Administration
Agency Building
4 Empire State Plaza, 20th Floor
Albany, NY 12223
518-474-1038;
270 Broadway
New York, NY 10007
212-587-5900

Chief Judge of the Court of Appeals
Court Appeals Hall
Eagle Street
Albany, NY 12207
518-455-7720

ADMINISTRATIVE DEPARTMENTS AND OFFICES:

Department of Agriculture and Markets
Capitol Plaza
1 Winner's Circle
Albany, NY 12235
518-457-3880

Department of Audit and Control
Alfred E. Smith
Office Building
Albany, NY 12236
518-474-4015

Department of Banking
2 Rector Street
New York, NY 10016
212-618-6220;
194 Washington Avenue
Albany, NY 12210
518-474-2364

Department of Civil Service
State Campus (Building 1)
Albany, NY 12239
518-457-2487
Handicapped Employment:
1-800-635-6333

Department of Commerce
1 Commerce Plaza
Albany, NY 12245
518-474-1431

Department of Correctional Services
State Campus (Building 2)
Albany, NY 12226
518-457-7329

Department of Education
Education Building
Albany, NY 12233
518-474-1201

Department of Environmental Conservation
50 Wolf Road
Albany, NY 12233
518-457-5400

Department of Health
Empire State Plaza
(Tower Building)
Albany, NY 12237
518-474-5422;
518-474-7354

Department of Insurance
160 West Broadway
New York, NY 10013
212-602-0434;
Empire State Plaza
(Agency Building 1)
Albany, NY 12257
518-474-6600
General Information:
1-800-342-3736

Department of Labor
State Campus
(Building 12)
Albany, NY 12240
518-457-5519

Department of Law
State Capitol
Albany, NY 12224
518-474-7124

Department of Motor Vehicles
Empire State Plaza
(Swan Street Building)
Albany, NY 12228
518-474-0877

Department of Social Services
40 North Pearl Street
Albany, NY 12243
518-474-9516;
1-800-342-3715

Department of State
162 Washington Avenue
Albany, NY 12231
518-474-4764 -4750
Ombudsman:
1-800-828-2388
*Committee on Open
    Government:*
518-474-2518

**Department of Taxation
    and Finance**
State Campus
    (Building 9)
Albany, NY 12227
518-457-4242
Tax Information:
1-800-342-3536
Tax Publications:
1-800-462-8100
Tax Refunds:
1-800-443-3200

**Department of
    Transportation**
State Campus
    (Building 5)
Albany, NY 12232
518-457-6195

Public Service Commission
Empire State Plaza
    (Agency Building 3)
Albany, NY 12223
518-474-7080

SELECTED BIBLIOGRAPHY

Annual Report, New York State Commission on Judicial Conduct. New York, N.Y.: Commission on Judicial Conduct, 1985, 1986, 1987, 1988.

"Canon 7 of the Code of Judicial Conduct," *Tenth Annual Report, New York State Commission on Judicial Conduct.* New York, N.Y.: Commission on Judicial Conduct, March 1985. Adopted by the New York State Bar Association and the American Bar Association.

A Citizen's Guide to the APA (Adirondack Park Agency) Land Use Regulations. Albany, N.Y.: State of New York, Adirondack Park Agency, 1980. Pamphlet.

"Chronological Table of Principal New York Environmental Laws," *New York State Environmental Law Handbook 1987.* New York, N.Y.: New York State Bar Association, 1987.

The Citizen Lobbyist: A Guide to Action in Albany. New York, N.Y.: League of Women Voters of New York State, 1976. Revised edition, 1982.

The Courts of New York—A Guide to Court Procedures, with a Glossary of Legal Terms. New York, N.Y.: Committee on Courts and the Community of the New York State Bar Association, 1987. Pamphlet.

Factbook—June 1987. Albany, N.Y.: New York State Department of Environmental Conservation, June 1987.

Environment 2000. Albany, N.Y.: New York State Governor's Office, 1986.

Environmental Quality Bond Act 1986—Annual Report 1987. Albany, N.Y.: New York State Department of Environmental Conservation and New York State Office of Parks, Recreation, and Historic Preservation, 1987.

Facts for Voters. New York, N.Y.: League of Women Voters of New York State, 1987. Pamphlet.

Facts for Voters. New York, N.Y.: League of Women Voters of New York State, 1988. Pamphlet.

The Health Care Puzzle in New York State: A Citizen Guide. New York, N.Y.: League of Women Voters of New York State, 1985.

How a Bill Becomes a Law. New York, N.Y.: League of Women Voters of New York State, 1975.

The Judicial Maze. New York, N.Y.: League of Women Voters of New York State, 1988.

New York State: A Citizen's Handbook. New York, N.Y.: League of Women Voters of New York State, 1979, 1974, 1968, 1963, 1954.

New York State Department of Transportation Annual Report. Albany, N.Y.: New York State Department of Transportation, 1987.

New York State Forest Preserve—Centennial Fact Book. Albany, N.Y.: New York State Department of Environmental Conservation, 1985.

1989-90 Directory of New York State Officers and Officials. New York, N.Y.: League of Women Voters of New York State, 1989.

Rebuild New York. New York State Department of Transportation (DOT), 1987. DOT Regional Offices. Pamphlet.

The Road to the Voting Booth. New York, N.Y.: League of Women Voters of New York State, 1986.

"Rules Governing Judicial Conduct," *Tenth Annual Report , New York State Commission on Judicial Conduct.* Promulgated by the Chief Administrative Judge of the Unified Court System of the State of New York. New York, N.Y., Commission on Judicial Conduct, March 1985.

SPDES. . . Water Pollution Control in New York State. (Fresh Water Classification.) Albany, N.Y.: New York State Department of Environmental Conservation, December 1983.

State of New York 1988 Election Law. Albany, N.Y.: New York State Board of Elections, 1988.

A Tradition of Conservation. Albany, N.Y.: New York State Department of Environmental Conservation, January 1988.

Transportation 2000. Albany, N.Y.: New York State Department of Transportation, 1987.

GLOSSARY

absentee ballot: an official ballot used by a voter who is unable to go to the polls on Election Day because of absence or illness.

acid rain: precipitation that carries air pollution to the ground.

act: a law made by a governing body, such as a state legislature.

acquittal: a court's decision that an accused person is not guilty.

administration: the governor, governor's staff, and other officials who take leadership roles in the executive branch of government.

administrative law: rules and regulations issued by government agencies.

advisory opinion: an opinion by an attorney general regarding the constitutionality of a law.

affirmative action: a policy or program for correcting the effects of discrimination in the employment or education of members of certain groups, such as women, Blacks, and Hispanics.

amendment: a revision or addition proposed or made in a bill, law, or constitution.

annexation: the expansion of municipal boundaries to include a bordering area.

appellate jurisdiction: the right of a higher court to review a decision of a lower court.

apportionment: proportional distribution of the number of members of the U.S. House of Representatives, New York State Assembly, and New York State Senate, on the basis of population.

aquifer: underground geologic formations that store and transmit significant quantities of ground water.

arraignment: the formal reading in open court of charges against a defendant.

assembly: a body of lawmakers in state government; the Assembly is one of two houses in New York State government.

assessment: an estimate of the value of property for purposes of taxation.

assessor: a local government official who inspects property and estimates its value.

at-large: a system of election by which all voters of a city or town elect government officials.

attorney general: the chief legal officer of state government.

bail: money exchanged for release of an arrested person as guarantee of that person's appearance for trial.

bench trial: trial by a judge rather than by a jury.

bicameral: having two legislative houses.

bilingual education: classroom instruction in a student's native language as well as English.

bill: a proposed law that is being considered by a legislature.

bill of rights: constitutional list of the basic civil liberties of citizens.

bipartisan: consisting of or supported by members of two major parties.

block grant: a grant from the federal government channelling money to a state (or from the state to a local municipality) for general purposes.

board of elections: a governmental agency that monitors political elections to ensure that election laws are enforced.

board of equalization: a group established by a government to ensure fair property taxes.

bond: a loan to the government by private citizens or corporations.

brief: a written document presenting one side of a court case.

budget: a plan for spending money over a certain period of time; an itemized summary of expenditures and income for a given period.

bureaucracy: the agencies and offices that take part in managing the government.

calendar: a formal schedule of bills to be considered by a legislature; a schedule of cases to come before a court (also called a **docket**).

capital punishment: the death penalty.

caucus: a meeting of the members of a political party to nominate candidates to decide party policies.

census: an official count of the population.

charge: to accuse a person formally of an illegal act.

charter: a legal document granted by a state creating a government entity, a college, a bank, or a public authority.

checks and balances: a system under which each branch of government limits the power of the other branches.

chief executive: the official who runs or administers a government. The governor is the chief executive of New York State.

citizen: a person entitled by birth or naturalization to the protection of a government or a natior

citizenship: the special status, including rights and responsibilities, possessed by a person by virtue of birth or naturalization.

city manager: professional employed by a city council to oversee the city's operations.

civil law: the body of law that deals with the relations between people. Also called **private law.**

civil service: the system by which public employees are hired and promoted on the basis of merit rather than because of political party affiliation (the **"spoils system"**).

civil rights: the right of every citizen to be treated equally under the law and to have equality of opportunity.

code: a system of regulations and rules of procedure.

code of ethics: rules and guidelines for behavior of government officials.

collective bargaining: negotiations between a union and an employer to determine wages, hours, and working conditions.

commission: a group of people officially authorized to perform certain duties or functions.

committee: a group of legislators who meet to consider bills in a single area, for example, agriculture, appropriations, commerce, or election law.

comptroller: chief financial officer of the state.

constituency: the people whom elected officials represent and to whom they are directly accountable.

constitution: a document outlining the basic form and rules of a government.

convention: a formal meeting of members, representatives, or delegates of a group such as a political party.

council manager: a form of municipal government in which the voters elect a council to make policy, and the council appoints a manager to execute the policy.

county: a municipal corporation, established by the state legislature, with geographical jurisdiction, powers, and fiscal capacity to provide a wide range of services to residents.

county executive: an official, usually elected, who heads the executive branch of county government.

county manager: professional manager appointed by the governing board of a county to supervise day-to-day operations.

county seat: town or city that contains the county government's offices and buildings.

criminal law: the body of law that specifies offenses against the public and the penalties for committing those offenses.

debt limit: a constitutional borrowing limit placed on municipalities whereby they may borrow up to a set percentage of their assessed valuation of real property.

deficit: the amount by which a sum of money falls short of the required amount.

deficit spending: the practice of spending funds in excess of income, expecially by a government.

democracy: rule by the people.

district attorney: chief prosecuting attorney of a county or state; an elected official.

due process of law: fair and predictable procedures to ensure the fair treatment of those accused of crimes.

ecology: science of the relationships between organisms and their environment.

election district: basic unit of election administration, having no more than 950 registered voters in it; district lines are set by the municipality.

election: the act of selecting public officials by vote.

electorate: people who are legally eligible to vote in an election.

emissions: pollutants released into the air, especially by the internal combustion engines of automobiles, trucks, and buses.

enabling act: a provision added to a constitutional amendment authorizing the legislature to pass whatever laws are necessary to make the amendment effective.

endorsement: expressing public support for a candidate for political office.

equalization rate: a formula to create equity in tax rates among multiple units of local government when the assessed valuations bear a varying relationship to full value. This formula is used in county tax assessment and in school districts that cover more than one community.

executive: the branch of federal, state, or local government that is responsible for putting laws into effect. The chief executive of New York State is the governor.

executive budget: a state budget that is prepared under the direct supervision of the governor.

executive order: a rule or regulation issued by the governor to help enforce a law.

felony: a serious crime punishable by more than one year in prison.

fiscal policy: a governmental tool for influencing the economy by changing levels of taxing and spending.

fiscal year: the twelve-month period for which a government plans the use of its funds.

flat grant: the minimum amount of state aid to education given to all school districts regardless of their wealth.

fossil fuel: an energy source, such as coal, oil, or natural gas, formed millions of years ago from decomposed plants and animals.

franchise: the right to vote.

GAAP (General Accepted Accounting Principles): sets forth uniform minimum standards and guidelines for financial accounting and reporting.

general election: an election involving most or all voters of a state in selecting candidates and/or deciding ballot issues; held on the first Tuesday after the first Monday in November.

general welfare: the well-being of a society as a whole (see also **social welfare**).

gerrymander: setting district boundary lines to favor a particular candidate, political party, or group.

govern: to make and administer the public policy and affairs of state.

government: the people and institutions with the authority to establish and enforce laws and public policy.

governor: the chief executive of a state.

grand jury: a group of people who decide whether there is sufficient evidence to hold a person for a criminal trial.

grant-in-aid: monies given on a matching basis to a state or a local government by the national or state government for a particular program or project.

hand down: to announce or deliver.

Home Rule: the principle that a locality should have complete self-government of its internal affairs.

hydroelectric power: power produced by the energy of falling water (channelled through dams).

immunity: the promise of legal authorities that the testimony given by witnesses will not be used to prosecute them for crimes.

impeach: to accuse a public official, before an appropriate tribunal, of misconduct.

inalienable rights: rights that cannot be denied.

income tax: a tax on a person's income.

incumbent: a person who holds political office.

independent: a person who has not enrolled in a political party.

indictment: a formal statement presented by a prosecuting attorney charging a person with committing a crime.

inflation: a persistent, substantial rise in the general price level, resulting in a fall of purchasing power.

infrastructure: the basic installations and facilities, such as roads, bridges, schools, and transportation systems, of a community or state. **Infrastructure neglect** over several decades has led to the deterioration of some of these systems, and has necessitated costly repairs.

initiative: the procedure by which citizens can propose a law by petition and ensure its submission to the electorate.

interstate: pertaining to two or more states.

intrastate: pertaining to or existing within the boundaries of one state.

Jacksonian democracy: the movement toward greater citizen participation in government.

joint session: a session in which both legislative houses meet together.

judge: a public official authorized to make decisions on cases of law.

judicial: the branch of government that decides if laws have been broken and that punishes lawbreakers.

judicial review: the power of the courts to decide whether certain laws and acts of governmental officials are consistent with the ideas of the constitution.

jurisdiction: authority vested in the court to hear certain cases.

labor: the human resources needed to produce goods and services.

law: all the rules of conduct established by a government and applicable to a people, whether in the form of legislation or of custom.

legislative: the branch of government that makes laws.

legislator: a person who makes or votes on laws; a member of a legislative body.

legislature: the lawmaking branch of government.

lobbyist: a representative of an organization or group that has attempts to influence laws.

logrolling: practice by which lawmakers agree to vote for each other's bills.

magistrate: a minor official with limited judicial powers, such as a justice of the peace or judge of a police court.

majority rule: the principle by which people agree to abide by decisions on which more than half of them agree.

mandate: the wishes or support of the people as expressed by their vote.

mass media: sources of information, including radio, television, newspapers, and magazines, that influence a large number of people.

mass transit: a system of moving people from place to place by public conveyance such as train, bus, ferry, or subway.

mayor-council: a form of municipal government in which the voters elect both a mayor and a council to govern.

Medicaid: joint federal-state program to aid the poor in paying for medical expenses.

Medicare: federal social insurance program for those over 65.

merger: combining of two or more entities, as in court merger—the combining of trial courts.

merit employment: the practice of hiring and promoting employees on the basis of objective, unbiased, competitive testing.

message of necessity: a message from the governor to the legislature requesting an immediate vote on a bill.

misdemeanor: a lesser crime, generally punishable by less than one year in prison.

moral obligation bonds: provision in an authority's enabling act that requires the state to restore any deficiencies in the fund supporting the bonds.

municipality: a political unit, such as a town, city, or village, incorporated for local self-government.

nominating convention: the meeting of party delegates in a gubernatorial or presidential election year to nominate candidates and to write a platform.

nomination: the process of proposing or naming a candidate for elective office.

nonrenewable: a natural resource that is depleted with use.

nuclear power: the power produced from the energy released by an atomic reaction.

original jurisdiction: the authority of a court to hear and to decide a case for the first time.

override: the power of a legislature to pass a law after the executive (governor) has vetoed it.

pardon: an executive order that frees a person from punishment or legal consequences of a crime.

petit jury: also called **trial jury**. A group of impartial people who evaluate evidence and determine an accused person's guilt or innocence.

petition: a formal request signed by a number of citizens and addressed to a government or other authority.

pigeonhole: to kill a bill by refusing to take action on it or pass it out of committee.

platform: a political party's declaration of principles and policies.

plea bargaining: a practice in which a criminal defendant is, under certain conditions, allowed to plead guilty to a lesser charge without a trial, usually resulting in a lenient sentence.

plurality: highest number of votes.

political action committee (PAC): a legal entity set up by a special-interest group to collect and spend funds for a political purpose.

political party: an organization of citizens who work together to elect candidates and to set public policy.

politics: participation in political affairs.

pre-file: to file a bill before the regular legislative session begins.

presidential primary: a party election in which voters choose the candidate they want their convention delegates to nominate.

primary: an election to determine the nominees of a political party. In New York State, a voter must be enrolled in a political party to vote in the party's primary.

probable cause: reasonable grounds for believing that a crime has been committed and that the person arrested is the one who committed it.

quota: a required or assigned percentage.

quorum: a minimum number of members of a group required to conduct business.

ratification: a process for formally approving a law, treaty, or constitution.

property tax: a tax imposed on real or personal property.

prosecuting attorney: the government's legal representative who brings charges and attempts to prove a crime has been committed.

public assistance: aid programs funded by federal and state dollars available to those who can prove they are in need.

public defender: an attorney employed by the state and appointed by the court to defend persons unable to afford legal assistance.

public domain: owned by the public; not subject to copyright law.

public law: part of the legal system that deals with the relationship between government and its citizens.

public utility: a company supplying gas, electricity, or water to the public under the oversight of an agency of the government.

real property: land, including the buildings or improvements on it, and its natural assets.

reapportionment: the redistribution of representation in a legislative body according to changes in the census figures.

recess: a brief period during which the legislature is not in session.

recession: a mild, short-term economic slump.

redistrict: to redraw the boundaries of legislative districts.

referendum: the submission of a proposed law to the vote of the electorate.

registration: the act of formally entering one's name on the election rolls by swearing that one is a citizen, eighteen years of age or older, and a resident of the election district for the requisite amount of time.

regulation: a rule by a government agency or department for the purposes of enforcing a law.

regulatory agency: an administrative part of government that carries out laws.

renewable: a resource that can be replaced, such as timber.

representative: a person who represents a constituency in a legislative body; a member of Congress.

representative democracy: a form of government in which a small group of people is elected to act for or on behalf of a constituency in exercising a voice in legislation.

reserved powers: powers of the the states. Those powers that the U.S. Constitution neither gives to the national government nor denies to the states.

residency: a requirement that voters must live in an election area for a certain amount of time before they are eligible to vote there.

revenue: income of a government from all sources appropriated for the payment of public expenses.

revenue sharing: a form of government financing by which a portion of money collected in federal income tax is returned to the state and local government.

right-to-work law: a state law which allows a person to obtain and to keep a job without joining a labor union.

save harmless: a provision of the financing of public school law that states that a district will not receive less state aid than it did in the previous year.

school board: locally elected or appointed body that governs a school district.

school district: an area within a state defined by state government to administer the public schools of that area.

senate: a body of lawmakers in government. The "upper house" of the New York State legislature.

sentence: punishment decided by a court.

separation of powers: division of the legislative, executive, and judicial functions of government into three branches.

sheriff: the chief representative of the courts in certain counties.

small claims court: minor court that hears civil cases involving small amounts of money, usually no more than $2000.

solid waste: garbage and trash.

special district: a unit of local government set up to provide services which a local government does not provide, such as fire protection and water supply.

special session: legislative session called by the governor and limited to subjects put forth by the governor.

sponsor: a member of the legislature who introduces a bill.

state: an independent political unit characterized by population, territory, government, and sovereignty.

state of the state: the constitutionally required annual report of the Governor of New York State to the legislature outlining the government's past accomplishments and future goals.

subpoena: a court order requiring a person to appear as a witness.

sunshine law: a law requiring government agencies to hold open meeings and to to give advance notice of these meetings.

table: a parliamentary motion to "kill" a bill.

tax base: the total assessed value of all property in a community.

toxic waste: the hazardous and often poisonous byproducts of chemical manufacturing.

three-day rule: requires that bills awaiting passage by either house must sit three legislative days before a final vote may be taken.

true bill: a grand jury's agreement with a prosecutor that the evidence warrants a trial.

two-party system: a political system in which two major groups with differing political philosophies compete for control of the government.

unalienable right: see inalienable right.

unconstitutional: pertaining to a law not allowed by the constitution.

unemployment compensation: a government payment under the Social Security Act to persons who lose their jobs through no fault of their own.

urban renewal: the improving or rebuilding of declining downtown areas of cities.

user's fee: a revenue collected for consumption of a service, such as metered water or electricity.

union: an association of people or states that join together for a common purpose.

venue: location of a trial.

veto: power of a chief executive to prevent a bill from becoming a law. A veto may be **overridden** by a vote of the legislature.

will: a legal document made by a person directing what should be done with his or her property after the person's death.

withholding: an automatic deduction from wages or salary used to prepay income tax.

worker's compensation: payments required by law to be made to an employee who is injured or becomes ill on the job.

write-in candidate: a candidate whose name does not appear on the ballot and whose name must be written on the ballot by supporters.

zoning: regulations for use or occupancy of land.

INDEX

Accelerated Capacity and Transportation
  Improvements of the Nineties Bond Act   142
Accounting, Financial Reporting and
  Budget Accountability Reform
  Act of 1981   7, 58
Administrative Board   27, 31
Albany Mall   69
Anderson v. Regan   7
Arab oil embargo   3
Attorney General   17
Attorneys   33-34

Big Five Cities   86, 103
Bills   47-54
  Action by the Governor   53
  Counting the vote   52
  Fast roll call   52
  How a bill becomes a law   47-54
  Introduction   47
  Message of Necessity   52
  Obstacles to progress   50
  "Party Bills"   51
  Passing   51-52
  Progress   49
  Rules Calendar   52
  Schedule for introducing   49
  Slow roll call   52
  Starred bills   51
Blaine Amendment   10
Board of Elections   154-155
  Local boards   155
  New York State board   154-155
Board of Regents   106, 107
BOCES   108-109
Borrowing   64
"Bottle Bill"   131
Budgets   55-65
Balanced budget mandate   58
  Deficiency   58
  Major planning   58
  Supplemental   58
  What budget pays for   60-64
Budget making process   55-58

Campaign finance laws   148
Campaign financing   160-162
Campaign financing limits   163

Candidates   160
Candidate selection   150
  Independent nominations   151
  Nominations to statewide office   150
Certificate of Participation (COP)   69
Chief Administrator   30-31
Cities   84-89
  Big Five   85, 103
  History   84, 87
  Number of   84
  Types of government   84-85
City University of New York (CUNY)   109
Civil Service Law   166
Code of Judicial Conduct   162
Collective bargaining   121
Commission of Judicial Nomination   27
Commissioner of Education   107
Comprehensive Employment Training
  Act (CETA)   120
Comptroller   17-18
Conservation policies   3
Constitution   8-12
  Amendments   8
  Articles   12
  Bill of Rights   9
  Convention   9-10
  Court system   6
  1894 document   9
  History and trends   3-8
  Limits and inconsistencies   11
  Tax structure changes in 1970s   3
Constitutional amendments   53-54
Counsel for the indigent   34
Counties   81-84
Charter   82-83
  History   81
  Home Rule Act   83
  Officials   83
  Responsibilities   82, 84
Court Administration   30-31
Court Financing   31-32
Court Merger   12
Court structure and jurisdiction   19-25
Courts
  Appellate Courts   19-22
  Appellate Division   21
  Appellate Division of Supreme Court   22

City Courts outside New York City	25
Civil Court of City of New York	25
Court of Appeals	19-22
County Court	23
Court of Claims	24
Criminal Court of City of New York	25
District Courts	24
Family Court	23
Local trial courts	24-25
New York City Courts	25
Supreme Court	23
Surrogate's Court	24
Town and Village Courts	25
Trial courts	23-24
Deficiency appropriation	58
Department of Audit and Control	17
Department of Education	108
Department of Law	17
Dormitory Authority	68
Education	103-109
Aid	104, 106
State share	106
Capital Construction	106
Board of Education	105
Factors affecting	103-104
Financing	104, 106
Cities	104
School districts	95, 105
School budgets	105
School elections	105
State Local Relationships	108
State Structure of Education	107
Transportation	105
Educational Conference Board	106
Election districts	158
Elections	153-162
Absentee Voting	162
Election Day procedures	158-159
General Elections	157
Poll Hours	159
Primaries	158
School elections	105, 158-159
Types in New York State	157-158
Village elections	158
Environment	125-137
Environmental Conservation,	
Department of	125-137
Administration	125
Air resources	126-127
Division of Construction Management	129
Division of Water	129
Ground Water Protection	129

Quality Classifications	129-130
Regulatory process	136
Water, Rivers and Streams	129
Environmental Conservation	
Laws (ECLs)	136
Environmental impact statement	136
Environmental Quality Bond	
Act (EQBA)	131,134
Equalization and assessment	79-80
ESL	104
Ethics Law	167-168
Executive branch	13-18
Executive sessions	170
Fair campaign code	164
Finance	55-69
Division of the Budget	56
Role of the governor	55-56
Fire Services	98-99
Fire Districts	98
Fire Protection Districts	98-99
History	99
Fiscal Year	57
Fish and Wildlife, Division of	133
Flat Grants	106
Fleischmann Commission Report	103
Freedom of Information Law	6, 165, 166
Fresh Water Wetland Act	134
General Fund	
What budget pays for	60-64
Allocations	60, 63
Government changes in 1980s	7
Governor	13-16
Appointment	15
Budget-making role	14, 55-56
Executive and administrative powers	14-15
Impeachment	13
Qualifications	13
Legislative powers	15
Limitations	16
Political role	16
Pardoning power	14-15
Succession	18
Health Care	4-5, 62
Health, Department of	113-115
Helen Hayes Hospital	114
New York State Veterans' Hospital	
in Oxford	115
Office of Health Systems Managemnt	
(OHSM)	114
Office of Public Health (OPH)	113-114
Roswell Park Memorial Institute	114

Highway Act of 1909   137
Highway construction   4, 62
Home rule   11, 83
Home Rule Article,
   See Muncipal Home Rule Board   39, 73, 83
Housing   122-123
   Division of Housing and Community
Renewal   122
     History   122
     Housing Task Force   123
     New innovations in housing   124
     New York State Housing Finance
      Agency   122
     State of New York Mortgage Agency
      (SONYMA)   122
Housing Finance Agency   68
Housing Law of 1926   122

Improvement Districts
   (Special Districts)   99-100
   County   99
   Town   99-100
Income and expenditures,
   New York State   58-60
Income wealth   103

Job Training Partnership Act (JTPA)   120
Judges
   Appellate Division Justices   27
   City Court Judges Outside New York City   29
   County Court Judges   28
   Court of Claims Judges   29
   District Court Judges   29
   Family Court Judges   29
   Judge of Court of Appeals   27
   Judges of the Court of Appeals   27
   New York City Civil Court Judges   29
   New York City Criminal Court Judges   30
   Qualifications and Terms of Office   26-30
   Retirement of Judges and Justices   30
   Supreme Court Justices   28
   Surrogate Court Judges   29
   Town and Village Court Justices   29
Judicial Branch   19-38
Judicial Campaign   164
Judicial Department   19
Judicial Discipline   32-33
Judicial District Conventions   28
Judicial Selection   26-30
Juries   34
   Enforcement   38
   Disqualifications   37
   Fees   38
   Grand   34-35
   Qualifications   36
   Trial juries   35-36

Labor, Department of   118-122
   Department of Civil Services   118
   Division of Human Rights   120-121
   Job Services Training   119-120
   Organization   118
   Public Employee Relations
     Board (PERB)   118
   Standards and Wages   119
   Unemployment   119-20
   Working Conditions   119
Labor Relations Act   121
Lands and Forests, Division of   134
   Adirondack Park Agency (APA)   134
   Pesticide Management   134-135
Lawyer's Code of Professional
   Responsibility   33
Lease Purchase   69
Legislators   40-41
   District Representation   39
   Salaries   41
Legislature   39-46
   As coequal partner with executive branch   7
   Committees   44-46
   Finance Committees   46
   Officers   43-44
   Organization   43-46
   Powers and limitations   39-40
   Rules Committee, key role   45
   Sessions   41-42
Lieutenant-Governor   16-17
Lobbying Regulations   171
Local government   72-93
   Federal and state aid   76
   History   72
   Local-State fiscal relationships   74-75
   Local-State administrative relationship   80-81
   Municipal Annexation Law   74
   Muncipal Home Rule Law   73
   Other taxes   78
   Rights and powers   73
   Statute of Local Governments   73
Low Level Radioactive Waste
   Management Act   136

Marine Resources, Division of   135
Mental health   5, 62
Mental Hygiene   115-118
   Division of Alcoholism and
     Alcohol Abuse   116-117
   Division of Substance Abuse Services   117-118
   Office of Mental Health Services   115

Office of Mental Retardation and
  Development Disabilities
  (OMRDD)   115-116
Merit selection system for judges   26
Merit systems for civil service   7
Metropolitan Transportation Authority   68
Mineral Resources, Division of   135
Moreland Act Commission   15

Natural Resoures Management   133
New York City   86-89
  Board of Estimate   87
  Budgets   87-88
  Charter   87
  City Council   87
  Community Boards   88
  Financial Control Board   88
  Mayor   87
  Schools   89
New York State Board of Equalization
  and Assessment   79
New York State Board of Law Examiners   33
New York State Commission on
  Judicial Conduct   32-33
New York State County Law   82
New York State Election Law   147, 148
New York State Inactive Hazardous Waste
  Site Remedial Plan   132
New York State Power Authority   68
New York State Returnable Beverage
  Container Act   131
New York State Social Security Agency   18
New York State Thruway Authority   68
New York State Town Law   89
New York State Village Law   91

Occupational Safety and Health
  Act (OSHA)   119
Office of Court Administration   37
One man, one vote   10, 39, 83, 87, 145
Open Meetings Law   6, 165-167
Organized Crime Task Force   17

PACS   163
Permanent personal registration   158
Political Parties   145-151
  County commitee   148-149
  Election districts   147-148
  Enrollment   147
  Local party committees   148
  Organization   147
  Organization in New York City   149
  Recognized parties   146
  State committee   149

Weakening of the two party-system   146
Port Authority of New York
  and New Jersey   68
Property tax   5-6, 75-76, 79-80, 103
Property wealth   103
Public authorities   66-68, 100
Public Authorities Control Board   68
Public Employees Safety and Health Act   119
Public Tranportation Safety Board   138

Real Property Tax Law   79
Rebuild New York Transportation
  Infrastructure Renewal Bond Act   142
Registration procedures   156-157
Regulatory Affairs, Division of   136
Return a Gift to Wildlife Program   133
Revenues, state, 10 year growth   59, 61
Ruben Commission Report   103
Rules Governing Judicial Conduct   164

Save harmless   106
School Administration on the Local Level   105
Schools, see Education
School Districts, Number   103
Social Services   4-5, 111-113
Social Services, Department of   111
  Aid to Families with Dependent
    Child (AFDC)   112
  Food Stamp Program   112
  Home Relief (HR)   112
  Homeless Housing and
    Assistance Program   113
  Medicaid   112
  Supplemental Security Income (SSI)   112
Solid Waste Management Plan   131
State Environmental Quality Review Act
  (SEQRA)   125, 136
State Implementation Plan (SIP)   126
State Mediation Board   121
State of the State   15
State Pollution Discharge
  Elimination System   129
State University of New York   109

Taxpayer's movement   6
Taylor Law   122
Tax Reform Act of 1987   57
Temporary State Commission on Regulation
  of Lobbying   171
Temporary State Commission
  on the Distribution of State Aid
  to Local School Districts   103
Towns   89-91
  Budget   90

189

History 89
Number 89
Structure and Officials 90
Town-Villages 92
Transportation, Department of 137-142
Administration 139
Airports 140
Canal System 141
Financing Improvements 141
History 137
Ports 141
Public Transit 138
Railroads 140
Waterways 141
Tri-State Planning Commission 92

Unified Court Budget Act 31
Uniform Procedures Act 136
Urban Development Corporation 68

Villages 91-92
History 91
Number 91
Structure and Powers 91
Voters
Administration 156
Qualifications 156
Who Cannot Vote 156

Waste 130-132
Hazardous Substances Division 131
Solid 131
Waste remediation 131
Wild, Scenic and Recreation River
System Act 134
Workers' Compensation Law 120

ABOUT THE LEAGUE OF WOMEN VOTERS
OF NEW YORK STATE AND
THE FOUNDATION FOR CITIZEN EDUCATION

THE LEAGUE OF WOMEN VOTERS OF NEW YORK STATE, founded in 1919, is a nonpartisan, nonprofit organization, composed of a strong network of 10,000 members in 78 local Leagues, that works to promote political responsibility through the informed and active participation of citizens in government. Although the League does not support or oppose any political party or any candidate, it does support or oppose certain legislation after serious study and substantial agreement among its members. Because of this program of legislative advocacy, the League of Women Voters of New York State is designated by the Internal Revenue Service as a tax-exempt nonprofit organization in accordance with Section 501(c)4 of the Internal Revenue Code.

THE FOUNDATION FOR CITIZEN EDUCATION, the tax-deductible affiliate of the League of Women Voters of New York State, was established in 1950. The Foundation is incorporated under the Not-for-Profit Corporation Law of New York and is classed as a public educational and charitable organization under Section 501(c)3 of the Internal Revenue Code. It works closely with local Leagues of Women Voters in New York State to support their citizen education projects. It conducts the citizen information activity of the League of Women Voters of New York State. The officers and directors of the League of Women Voters of New York State also serve as officers and directors of the Foundation for Citizen Education.